Cinderella Revisited

How to Survive
Your Stepfamily Without
a Fairy Godmother

Cinderella Revisited

How to Survive Your Stepfamily Without a Fairy Godmother

DR. PETER MARSHALL

To Diane

Thank you for making the daily 'rounds' so enjoyable. Perhaps we'll meet again next year

Peter.

Whitecap Books
Vancouver/Toronto

Edited by Elaine Jones
Cover and interior design by Warren Clark
Printed and bound in Canada

Canadian Cataloguing in Publication Data
Marshall, Peter Graham, 1947-
    Cinderella revisited

    Includes bibliographical references and index.
    ISBN 1-55110-094-0

    1. Stepparents. 2. Stepfamilies. 3.
    Parenting. I. Title.
HQ759.92.M37 1993   306.874   C93-091533-X

To my special friend and brother, West.

Acknowledgements

Guilt at having almost deserted my family to write my first book led me to publicly undertake to give all the royalties to my wife, Kathy. I feel compelled to make this a trend, although this time I am motivated more by appreciation than guilt. While I never promised her an easy life in front of witnesses, I did not realize how much she was taking on when she became a wife and a stepmother on the same day. Writing this book has convinced me that I owe her far more than I have acknowledged or can hope to repay adequately.

Contents

Foreword

Writing this book has proved to be a very personal experience. As a member of a stepfamily I find myself continually in the process of trying to "get it right." Putting my thoughts down about the stresses and strains of stepfamily life has reminded me of the times when I wondered if we would survive. Offering suggestions as to how people might approach issues and deal with problems has also made me aware of the occasions on which I should have been more diligent in putting my beliefs into practice. But another part of the experience has been far more positive. It has been reassuring to find that it is not hard to justify the position that stepfamilies can be strong and rewarding. The negative press that stepfamilies often seem to attract has tended to give them a poor reputation that overshadows the fact that they can be very successful.

The book incorporates three perspectives. The first is based on my experiences in a stepfamily. As I include references to our family in the book, I would like to introduce its other members—Kathy, my wife, Joanne and Tim, our children from my previous marriage, and Aaron, Kiera, and Alexandra, our children from our marriage.

The second perspective is that of a clinical psychologist who works with children and families. There was a time when families tended to see themselves as having failed in some way if they sought outside help. Fortunately, this attitude is less prevalent today and counseling and therapy have become more acceptable as ways of dealing with the difficult phases of stepfamily life. Perhaps because of my own history, I have derived particular pleasure and satisfaction from working with stepfamilies. Many have also taught me a great deal through sharing their successes and setbacks. I have included reference to some of these families, changing details only to ensure confidentiality.

The third perspective is more academic. Social scientists have played a major role in increasing our understanding of stepfamilies. I have discussed a number of their studies, as these provide insights into such topics as the way relationships with stepparents evolve, the role of the noncustodial parent, and the impact of being in a stepfamily on children's self-esteem and academic performance. The more information is gathered, the more the myths and fallacies about stepfamilies are eroded. The research also offers ideas about how to avoid or tackle the problems that families can face.

I have always argued that people in my profession should be seen as consultants rather than as experts who can necessarily prescribe solutions for a particular problem. If mental health professionals were that clever, I would be a lot richer and I could bore you endlessly with accounts of how my own stepfamily has lived in a state of perpetual bliss and harmony. In the absence of this recipe for success, I have been careful to emphasize that the recommendations contained in the book should be treated as no more than suggestions people may wish to consider. I often use the term *starting point*. As the term denotes, a starting point is intended to be an initial way of approaching an issue, be it the stepparent's role in discipline, how to involve stepgrandparents, or the method of organizing finances in the family. Some people may find the suggestions to be readily applicable to their situation; others, may want to modify them to take account of their family's particular circumstances.

Finding the right label to describe relationships has been difficult and there have been times when I have opted for simplicity at the expense of completeness or strict accuracy. I have used the term *biological* parent rather than always stating biological or adoptive parent. I have also referred to the parent who has primary responsibility for the children after a marital separation as the *custodial* parent. The ex-spouse in this situation is referred to as the *noncustodial* parent. In some families, however, I recognize that the parent who does not have the responsibility of day-to-day care of the children can still have legal guardianship through a joint custodial order.

I hope I have come close to reaching my two objectives as an author. The first was to provide a book that stepfamilies would find relevant and useful. The second was to maintain an optimistic and sometimes light-hearted approach without trivializing the subject matter. My optimism is based on the belief that the potential rewards of a stepfamily are considerable, even though there may be days when the fact that your decision to become part of the family was voluntary seems like one of life's unsolved mysteries. Searching for the humor reflects my refusal to ever take myself too seriously, and my belief that the capacity to smile or even laugh hysterically can prove to be the trusted defense mechanism that all members of a stepfamily need from time to time.

1

What is a Family, Anyway?

I doubt that I was exactly what my in-laws had in mind for their daughter. I hasten to add that I have never resented this; they are fine people whose tastes and preferences are beyond reproach. After all, name one parent you know who has said, "When you grow up try to marry a divorced man with children so that you can become a stepmother on your wedding day." So when Kathy told her parents she was dating a single father, I can appreciate why signs of apprehension, shock, and dismay were obvious, while indications of acceptance and enthusiasm were not. Her parents have always placed great value on education and the fact that I had a Ph.D. helped, but they would have gladly settled for a B.A. and no kids.

Most of us have grown up with the idea that a normal family consists of a mother and father, plus one or more offspring. The question "What is a family?" would not have been asked a generation ago. Of course, there were exceptions to the nuclear family. Death, and sometimes divorce, led to single-parent homes and stepfamilies. But these situations were very much exceptions; the two-parent, biological family ruled supreme as the model of family life. When we were young and fantasized about our futures, most of us saw ourselves continuing to live in a nuclear family, only as the parents rather than the children.

Then the divorce rate skyrocketed. Estimates vary, but anywhere from one-third to almost one-half of marriages can be expected to fail. Another way of describing the changes that have occurred is by referring to the statistics directly concerning children. For example, almost half of the children born in the eighties will spend at least part of their childhood in a single-parent family. As for stepfamilies, the projection is that approximately one-third of children can expect to be part of such homes by the turn of the century. Whatever statistic is used, the conclusion has to be that the nuclear family no longer has such an exclusive, dominant role in society.

Describing the types of families that are now commonplace is not a simple matter. The term *nuclear family* has already been used in reference to families in which there are parents living together who are both related to the children, either biologically or through adoption. Sometimes such families are also labeled "intact." I prefer not to use this term as it seems to suggest the other types of families are necessarily inferior. One dictionary definition of intact is "unimpaired." While my family life has not been without its fair share of problems and aggravations, I refuse to accept the idea that it has been impaired for the last eighteen years.

A *single-parent family* is obviously a household that includes only a mother or father. Children from single-parent families have been referred to as coming from "broken homes." This is another one of those labels I would like to see abandoned because of the implication of unavoidable inferiority. The number of single parents has risen steadily over the past few decades. There has also been a shift in the proportion of fathers who have custody of the children. It used to be assumed that the mother would have primary responsibility for childcare. Although most single-parent families continue to be headed by mothers, the percentage of single fathers rose to 10 percent in the eighties and is expected to rise.

While defining nuclear and single-parent families is straightforward, describing a *stepfamily* is an entirely different matter. It is tempting to provide a simple definition; for example, any family in which a biological parent has remarried. This would be accurate, but would not do justice to the many varieties of stepfamily that exist. A stepparent may live with the children; she could be married to the noncustodial parent and only see the child during access. The arrival of a stepparent could also bring stepsiblings into the picture. When the stepparent brings his or her children into the home, the term *blended family* is often used. In other families, the stepparent's children will be living with their other parent. Then there is the prospect that the biological parent and stepparent will have children of their own. If it happens that both already have children, the "mine, yours, and ours" family is created in which there are full, half-, and stepsiblings. Finally, the custody of the biological siblings can vary. In the majority of situations biological siblings are kept together, but the family or court may decide that it would be better for one to be with the mother while the other is raised by the father.

Idle curiosity once led me to calculate the number of possible permutations of stepfamilies. By the time I reached forty-eight I decided it was time to quit. The fact that a labeling system for the different types could not be accomplished by using even all the letters of the alphabet brought home the complexity of trying to describe the range of stepfamilies. I could refer to each one by a lengthy title, but a chapter headed, "The resident as well as nonresident stepparent, nonresident stepsibling, resident half-sibling, and biological siblings together stepfamily" would lack reader appeal.

Out of necessity I have returned to the simple definition of a stepfamily. But I hope that I have also communicated an appreciation that one person's stepfamily may bear little resemblance to another's, and that it would never be possible, therefore, to prescribe a single approach to family life or a simple solution for problems that may develop.

Before leaving the vocabulary to be used, I want to mention the label *reconstituted*. Apart from the fact that it immediately conjures up images of orange juice, it does not seem to fit the reality of stepfamily life. It denotes a rebuilding process, implying that remarriage is somehow putting pieces together in an effort to copy the nuclear family. I do not believe this is what happens; furthermore, as will be discussed in later chapters, the expectation that it will can lead to a lot of frustration and disappointment.

Much of my working life is spent listening to children. I am frequently reminded that many of them do not see families in the way my generation did. I often find myself becoming confused as the child makes reference to different family members. Sometimes it is hard to know if "mom" refers to a biological parent or stepparent, or if a brother is a step-, half-, or full sibling. I remember a ten-year-old girl becoming somewhat exasperated with me as I interrupted her to clarify who was who in her account of family life. Sarah was an engaging, no-nonsense child who commandeered pencil and paper so that she could spell it out for me. "It's really quite simple," she said with a noticeably condescending air. She drew the outline of a house and listed the people who were there when she was born. This was followed by a series of pictures, each one representing the family at key stages—for example, after her parents separated and when her father and, subsequently, mother remarried. By the time the lesson was over we had five pictures and the list of people she included in her family had gone from three to fourteen. It became obvious that she did not see family structure as static. She did not have a single mental image or model of a family; to her, a family was something that could change dramatically and could do so more than once. Like a number of her peers, she had experienced a nuclear family, single-parent family, and stepfamily, and had done so before reaching the midpoint of her childhood.

Sarah also highlighted another way in which children's views of family life can be at odds with their predecessors'. The nuclear family almost always constituted a home. Mom, dad, and children lived together and so the answers to the questions "who's at home?" and "who are the people in your immediate family?" would be the same. When you are part of a stepfamily, life isn't so simple. The emotional attachment to a newly acquired stepparent or stepsibling may be minimal, while the bond with a noncustodial parent can remain very strong. For Sarah, as well as many other children I have encountered, their family consisted of some, but not all of the people they lived with, as well as some, but not all of the people living in other households.

There is yet another way in which the generations can differ. In nuclear families, those living in the home are likely to share the same perception of who is and is not a core member. As a child, my immediate family included my parents and brother, West. I can remember times when I know West would have gladly sold me into slavery, and on a few occasions he probably could have done so with my parents' blessing. But, for the most part, I like to believe that he also saw me as part of his nuclear family, along with our mother and father. Similarly, our parents would have both included each other, as well as ourselves. But if you are in a stepfamily, each person in the home can have a very different view of their primary attachments. At the time I met Sarah and her family she was living with her mother, stepfather, and stepsister. Her strongest attachments were unequivocally to her mother and biological father. Her stepsister, on the other hand, clearly saw her own father and her noncustodial mother as her immediate family. As for the stepfather, although he was endeavoring to become closer to Sarah, his strongest ties were understandably to his biological daughter and new wife. Similarly, Sarah's mother felt far closer to her husband and daughter than to other people in the family configuration.

I found Sarah's lesson to be useful. On a number of occasions I have taken the initiative for bringing out pencil and paper and asking children to document the chronology and complexity of their family. They seem to enjoy the exercise; it can be a refreshing change to be the teacher for once and it provides a nonthreatening way for them to begin to identify areas of family life that may be difficult and upsetting. For myself, it can be an important part of being able to work with a child; I have to be able to see family life and history through her eyes before I can hope to be effective as a counselor or therapist.

The increase in divorce has dramatically changed the way in which many children must see family life. For them, a family is far from being a constant, self-contained unit and they may have no personal experience or memory of what it is like to be in a nuclear family. If you are a stepparent, you are faced with a far more complicated situation than you may have anticipated. You have the task of trying to understand and accommodate the fact that your model of the family may be very different from that of your children or spouse. You may live in the same house, but you can become increasingly and sometimes painfully aware of the distinction between physical proximity and emotional closeness. Your view of family life may change. For example, as you get to know a stepson or daughter you may find yourself *feeling* they are part of your family; this feeling may not, however, be mutual.

Given the uniqueness and complexity of stepfamilies, members can find it especially hard to understand one another's views and feelings. Much of what is written about stepfamilies centers on learning and communicating, as well as appreciating how each person would answer the questions, "What is my family?" and "What do I hope my family will become?" In general, there are no single or simple answers to these questions. For stepfamilies, the questions are especially complex. As I conceded, my in-laws had a point. While life in a nuclear family can, of course, become complicated, life in a stepfamily is guaranteed to be so. Fortunately, my wife-to-be did not appreciate the extent of this reality before she pledged her troth; the fact that so many single parents are able to remarry is heavily dependent on the power of love and romance to dull the senses and dampen the ability to foresee the consequences of one's actions.

2

Myths and Misconceptions

Expectations can have a powerful effect on how we feel and act. One example is how readily the failure to live up to the expectations we or others have of our performance can lead to feelings of disappointment and inadequacy. As a psychologist I have learned to make sure my limitations are known; sometimes it seems that people have too much confidence in our profession. At clinical meetings, for example, I often preface my report in such a way that everyone knows I can only address a few of the relevant questions. I find this approach to be far better than being faced with the prospect of giving a large number of consecutive, "I don't knows." I also make similar declarations socially. If anyone is so foolish as to ask me to dance, I insist we review the implications of such a venture in detail. I explain that the steps will have to be simple and highly repetitive, that I require leading, and that the chances of success will be greater if I can stay in forward gear. Once these understandings are in place, all that remains is for my partner to sign the personal injury waiver and off we go for a once-in-a-lifetime experience.

Life is much easier and far less frustrating when we do not have to be measured against unrealistic standards. Another type of expectation that causes problems is referred to as the "self-fulfilling prophecy." This refers to the idea that if we expect to find a task too difficult, this, of itself, increases the likelihood that we will fail. Conversely, if we anticipate that we will do well, this positive attitude can increase the likelihood of success. Much of the interest in self-fulfilling prophecies relates to education—for example, there are studies suggesting that one reason why certain students surpass others in achievement is simply that more is expected of them. There are, of course, limits to the power of self-fulfilling prophecies. I acted out my midlife crisis by taking saxophone lessons. My prophecy was that, in a few months, I would be auctioning off my couch and ink blots and wailing in a blues band. The fact that I am still in practice attests to the fact that expectations can—unfortunately—be overridden by a total absence of talent.

Myths associated with stepfamilies have the potential to become powerful expectations that can exert very negative effects on their members. The first two myths I will discuss relate to the extent to which expectations regarding the roles people should assume, and the type of relationships that should develop, can be unrealistic. For some stepfamilies, subscribing to these myths can become a guarantee of failure. The final myth is one that concerns the long-term success of stepfamilies and can become a negative self-fulfilling prophecy.

The Understudy Myth

This takes us back to the idea of reconstituting families: if one parent is absent, just find an understudy and the show will go on with the same script. As stepparents will know, it simply isn't and cannot be like that. Many will enter a stepfamily stating clearly and sincerely that they are not trying to take the place of the absent mother or father. Yet some find themselves acting as if they were replacement parts. After all, a stepfather is the only other adult in the home; parents are usually adults and, if you work on the assumption that there *should* be two parents present, he is the obvious candidate for the job. Furthermore, the second half of the title "stepfather" obviously seems to imply that he has agreed to shoulder at least some of the responsibilities of a parent.

It is not uncommon for stepparents to find themselves taking on a great deal of responsibility caring for children they are only in the process of beginning to know. I will be devoting a whole chapter to stepmothers and the particular myths and insults they have endured. For now, I will restrict my comments to the notion that becoming a "wicked stepmother" is often the result of having assumed the understudy role. The pressure to do so can be subtle; society has long had differing expectations for men and women when it comes to their obligations in families. The new wife can feel she should become very involved in the lives of her stepchildren. Her husband, on the other hand, may see her arrival as a golden opportunity to concentrate again on his career or recreational pursuits, safe in the knowledge that society remains relatively tolerant of men who take more of a backseat in family life.

Stepfathers are also vulnerable and again gender stereotyping is relevant. I can recall several stepfathers who have complained that they were expected to be the primary disciplinarians. Theory says that children secretly want structure and discipline and are truly grateful when we provide these. The reason this is largely a theory is that it is hard to find children who will publicly support it. No self-respecting daughter or son would ever admit to wanting to be told "no" after asking to go to an all-night party, and I can't recall even one occasion on which any of my five children has said, "By the way, Dad, I just wanted to say thank you for grounding me and taking away all my earthly privileges when I have broken the rules." While I believe children do appreciate discipline, they also resist it. This resistance can quickly become resentment and bitterness when the discipline comes from someone who may be living in the home, but has yet to become emotionally part of their family.

Entering a stepfamily means rewriting the script. Roles have to be negotiated, defined, and established. To what extent will a stepfather be seen as a parent, an older friend, or the mother's partner? The age of the children can be a crucial factor in deciding such issues. For an infant, it may be a relatively simple matter for a stepparent to begin taking an active role in day-to-day childcare. In all likelihood, the baby will accept this care readily from a stepparent just as he would from a babysitter. Older children, on the other hand, will vary considerably in their ability and willingness to allow a new parent-figure into their lives. Striving to establish a relationship as friends may be a more realistic route to take, at least initially.

Stepparents and stepchildren are not imitations of the "real thing"; they are unique family members. Often it is important to think carefully about abandoning preconceived notions of what a parent or sibling is supposed to be. Dispelling the understudy myth allows each person to start from scratch and begin to determine what role should be taken, given the needs and wishes of all family members.

The Instant-Love Myth

The unwritten rule-book for parents states that all mothers and fathers should not only love their children, but should love them equally. If you happen to feel closer to one of your children than another, you are supposed to keep this largely to yourself. I would not question the validity of such expectations for nuclear families; they would also apply to single parents. Too often, however, parents in stepfamilies try to utilize them as well. For very understandable reasons they want a close home-life, but find out all too soon that you can't just add a new parent, mix well, and have an instant loving family.

One particularly extreme example of the operation of the myth of instant love comes to mind. When Robert started to live with Cheryl and her four sons, the children were between the ages of six and eleven. He was a strict, somewhat authoritarian, but caring man. His view was that the three younger boys had accepted him almost immediately and that, even though they had lived together for only five months, they loved him, as he did them. He was puzzled, however, by the reaction of his oldest stepson, Paul, who was becoming increasingly withdrawn and had developed troubling symptoms such as stealing from family members. As I came to know the boys it was apparent that the notion of instant love was a major problem for the family. The three younger children did not, as yet, feel particularly close to Robert, but felt compelled to act as if they did. The bedtime ritual serves as an illustration. Every night Robert would tuck each boy into bed, read him a story, and kiss him goodnight, saying, "I love you, son." During a session with just the boys they talked about their mixed reactions to this. While they liked Robert and felt they should be grateful to him for all the interest he was showing in them, they didn't particularly want to kiss him or tell him they loved him. Each felt pressured in this situation, however, and had developed the practice of responding to, "I love you, son" with, "I love you too, dad." At some level they had become aware that this was expected of them, and their stepfather was adept at conveying the message that they should do what was expected. Saying, "I love you, dad" had become expedient, but it was not

13

heartfelt. It was also a lot simpler than, "I'm glad you think you love me, Robert, but I wonder if you aren't being somewhat premature. Speaking for myself, I feel I am just beginning to get to know you, but perhaps as time goes by we will become close and I will want to express affection openly with you."

Paul felt much the same toward his stepfather as did his brothers, but he was not willing to pretend it was otherwise. His belief that his brothers were very close to Robert, however, had led to his feeling increasingly left out. He was starting to wonder if there might be something seriously wrong with him that prevented his truly belonging to the family. Although it may sound paradoxical, the family became closer the more they were able to acknowledge that they were further apart than they had believed or pretended. Being open about the limits of their relationships was itself an exercise in developing the sensitivity and trust needed before genuine respect and affection could be present.

No more than a moment's reflection should be sufficient to dismiss the instant-love myth. How often do any of us experience such an automatic and strong bonding? Each time I tell the story of how I met my wife on a camping trip I change and embellish many of the details, but I always include the part where she first spied me, an Adonis-like figure silhouetted against the setting sun, and fell hopelessly and instantly in love. (Kathy also applies the word "hopeless" in her account of the meeting, but in a very different context.) But when I leave the realm of personal fantasy I am left with only the experience of childbirth as a credible example of instant love. I believe something unique and very special can happen when a parent first holds and cradles a child after birth. For many, the term instant love would be very appropriate, and in nuclear families the relationships with the children have the advantage of this strong bonding. Compare the experience of holding a newborn to that of picking your boyfriend up from his house and meeting his teenage daughter for the first time. While her, "Hi! nice to meet you" may sound reassuring, her tone and manner may be telling you, "Mess with my dad, lady, and I'll break your face." Both of you are probably experiencing strong and instant emotions, but love is unlikely to be one of them.

When a stepfamily is formed, it is critical not to have preconceived notions regarding how people should feel. Just as refusing to accept the understudy myth allows family members to decide for themselves what role they should play, dispelling the myth of instant love gives them license to accept how they are truly feeling without becoming guilty. The range of emotions people experience seems to expand the more I talk to stepfamilies. Dislike, confusion, ambivalence, indifference, caring, respect, resentment, and anxiety are just a sample.

The Second-Rate Myth

The term "step" comes from *stoep*, which means bereavement. It's certainly not an upbeat prefix and it has had negative connotations for many generations. As recently as 1976, for example, a definition of a stepchild was, "one who fails to receive proper care or attention." That's pretty insulting and unforgivably presumptuous, but it reflects the common myth that being in a stepfamily is, of necessity, second-rate. There may be an increasing acceptance of stepfamilies, but this does not necessarily mean that they are held in particularly high regard. For some people there is an assumption that stepchildren will inevitably fare less well than their counterparts in nuclear families; that there is something intrinsic to stepfamilies that makes them less effective. This is where the research is helpful. We certainly know that the vast majority of children are unhappy at their parents' separation. This is the case even when the parents report that the home life was poor for many years because of ongoing marital problems. The small minority of children who welcome their parents' separation tend to be those who have lived in an atmosphere of fear because of spousal or child abuse. In this respect, the research tells us what we would likely assume: most children would *prefer* to be in their original nuclear family. But does being in a family unit that is not at the top of your list of preferences mean that you will encounter significant problems in your life? Here the research is far more complicated. First of all, the results vary according to the particular area of development or adjustment being studied. Secondly, as so often happens in the social sciences, not everyone gets the same results even when they ask much the same question. An example is provided by the studies of self-concept. This is an important area, as children's ability to see themselves as worthwhile, likeable people and the self-confidence that such a perception permits are essential to healthy growth. Numerous studies have been conducted in which the self-concepts of children in nuclear families and stepfamilies have been compared. No consistent differences have emerged. One researcher may find that children from nuclear families score higher on measures of self-esteem; another may fail to find such a difference. Similarly, there is a lack of consistency in the research concerning academic achievement and general measures of personal adjustment. Furthermore, there have even been some studies indicating that stepchildren may be at an advantage with respect to social skills, perhaps because of their need to learn how to develop new and more complex relationships than typically exist in other families.

It is also important to keep in mind that, when studies have found a higher incidence of problems among stepchildren, the magnitude of the differences is typically small. No one should ever read research papers without remembering Mark Twain's, "there are lies, damned lies, and statistics." Not that social scientists set out to mislead people; the problem is one of how we care to represent their results. For example, Doctors Zimiles and Lee from Michigan studied over thirteen thousand students and found lower achievement scores and higher drop-out rates among students from stepfamilies. This way of describing the results could leave you with the feeling that being in a stepfamily condemns you to a life of ignorance and underachievement. Yet the same findings could be described in a way that would allow you to maintain a far more positive and optimistic outlook. As the researchers pointed out in their article, the achievement scores for students from nuclear families were higher by a "comparatively small margin." It was also true that, while students from stepfamilies were more likely to drop out, a substantial majority did not.

An interesting and important development in the research reflects a changing perception of the various types of family. The assumption that stepfamilies are necessarily inferior to the nuclear model is based on the idea that there is an underlying qualitative difference that has a negative influence on their functioning. The implication is that they are structurally flawed. Of course, the structure or arrangement of members in stepfamilies is different, as well as being relatively complex. As discussed in the previous chapter, you have the potential for the child's family to consist of step-, full, and half-relatives who live both in the home and in other households. If it is this type of structure in itself that is the problem, there is not too much you can do about it. Short of contacting the person you divorced and suggesting that you return to the altar, you can't re-create the nuclear family. Furthermore, as time goes by, stepfamilies often become more complicated and even less similar to the nuclear structure.

It is now evident from research, however, that simply being a member of a stepfamily does not impede children's development or adjustment. Attention has been directed towards finding out what happens in families (single-parent, nuclear, or step-) that influences children's well-being. The answers that have emerged tell us that stepfamilies have not cornered the market on a particular set of problems. Thomas and Jocelyn Parish are two social scientists who have conducted many studies of young people's self-esteem. One of their findings is that self-esteem is low when young people have experienced the parent as being hostile or uncaring. They found this to be true regardless of whether the person was in a stepfamily or nuclear family. In other studies, researchers have found that it is the degree of conflict and cohesiveness in families, rather than the structure of the family itself that relates to adjustment.

I find this type of research helpful. It can alert stepparents to potential risks and highlight the need to pay particular attention to certain aspects of family life. Stepfamilies are more likely to encounter family conflict and approximately one-quarter of stepchildren do perceive a parent as being hostile or uncaring. But these are problems that can be tackled by stepparents, just as they can when they occur in any other type of family. Believing in the second-rate myth results in people feeling stuck and inadequate; the more positive view of stepfamilies that emerges from the research allows parents to address problems in the knowledge that there may well be something they can do about them. Being in a stepfamily is not the same as being sentenced to life with no chance of parole. Stepfamilies are not by virtue of their existence second-rate. In the long run, stepfamilies can be very effective as a means of raising well-adjusted children, even though achieving this goal may be much harder and more stressful at times.

The last word should go to sociologist William Beer, who cited a number of studies relating to the long-term adjustment of stepchildren in his book, *American Stepfamilies*. At the end of his review of the research, he reassures us that "a stepfamily background is at most a minor obstacle to successful adult adjustment to family life, to emotional health, and to society at large."

3

Dealing With Children's Loss

Stepfamilies have been described as being "born of loss and hope." It may sound somewhat dismal to devote a chapter to loss, but I believe it is critical for parents in stepfamilies to appreciate the extent to which the children can be dealing with feelings of sadness and grief because of the changes that have occurred in their lives. Parents themselves may also be confronted with losses, but for now I would like to give center stage to the children and talk about the two areas that are likely to be most significant for them as they enter a stepfamily.

Loss of the Nuclear Family

Children's enjoyment of play can provide a valuable way of assessing how they feel about family life. One part of my practice is providing assessments for families who have separated and are trying to reach an agreement regarding custody of the children or visitation rights. During the individual sessions with children I often use play to construct their "dream house." We select miniature dolls to represent all the people in the family and proceed to use our imaginations to create the physical surroundings. A pencil becomes a magic wand and their enthusiasm builds as they add swimming pools, video-game arcades, or a cupboard full of their favorite junk food to their imaginary house. I then crown them prince or princess and tell them that they can either stay on their own with servants to take care of their every need or allow people into what has now become a palace to be envied. It is a rare occurrence for a child not to include both biological parents, and to do so without a moment's hesitation. What has been striking is that many children show the same response even when their parents separated many years previously. They may have been living in a stepfamily for quite some time, and could have established a very healthy relationship with the stepparent; there remains a part of them, however, that longs for the old family.

Parents may recognize that their child is still grieving the loss of the nuclear family, but sometimes they underestimate how strong the feelings can be. The reason seems to be that parents can often move ahead in their lives more readily than their children. There is almost always one partner who actively wanted and sought the divorce and whose strongest reaction to no longer being in the nuclear family will be relief. The other parent may feel much the same; if not, she or he will probably be able to come to terms with the separation and move on to a stage in which the relationship with the spouse is no longer a central part of their lives. But the children are in a very different position. Rarely do they want to "divorce" their parents. Their relationships with their mother and father are usually the strongest emotional attachments they have ever experienced and there is no motivation on their part to weaken these bonds. Even when there is a great deal of tension in the home because of marital conflict, children rarely perceive the separation as necessary or welcomed. It is only approximately 10 percent of children who express any positive feelings about the family breakup; this is usually in situations where they have been exposed to domestic violence.

When parents are looking ahead to new situations and relationships, it can be hard to recognize that their children are still looking over their shoulders and missing what they once had. This can also be one of those situations when children actually work too hard to please their parents. At some level they understand that they are supposed to have put the past behind them and should be getting on with their lives. So while their parents may tell me with sincerity that they believe their daughter has accepted the separation, she may be re-creating the nuclear family in a play session with me the next day and talking about how sad she feels that her dream house can only exist in fantasy.

Lee-Anne had reached the stage where she could reflect on the family history with objectivity and insight. She had been seven when her parents separated and she recalled a long period when she refused to believe they would not be getting back together. She would not tell her friends about what had happened and she made up elaborate stories to account for her father's absence and her spending every other weekend away from home. Somehow she seemed to believe that if she acted as if the family were still together, this would become true again. For her, reality struck home when her mother bought a book for her about divorce. They sat down together, and as she looked at the pictures and listened to her mother read of children becoming confused, angry, and sad when their parents divorced, she began to see herself in the pages and cried for the first time since the separation.

For Lee-Anne, acceptance of the separation was just the second stage. It took many more years before she abandoned the hope that, even though a legal divorce had occurred, her parents would come to their senses, love each other again, and remarry. By the time I first met her she had moved on to the stage where she had no illusions of a reconciliation. She was fifteen and laughed with genuine humor when I asked if she ever fantasized about her mother and father dating again. Yet, when I asked what was the hardest part of being in a separated family she stated simply, "Never having your mother and father with you together."

Children's feelings of loss do not mean they have to be stuck in the past. They too can adapt to change and come to terms with a situation they once refused to accept. A stepparent's arrival, however, can bring issues relating to grief and loss to the surface in a way that interferes with the process of establishing the new family. It is hard for a child to cling to the fantasy of his parents' getting back together when he is the ring-bearer watching his mother and prospective stepfather exchange vows. What is a day of happiness for them may be the death blow to his fantasies. As they head off for their honeymoon he might be tempted to ask, "I guess this means you and dad won't be getting back together?" but he already knows the answer.

I encourage parents to assume that the children are still experiencing feelings of loss, even if there are no obvious signs that this is so. I suggest that biological parents who are entering a new relationship take the time to talk privately with their children and explain that the old marriage is well and truly over and there would not have been a reconciliation even if the new partner were not in the picture. Being open about how people's feelings can be different is often another item on my list of recommendations. A parent can express her excitement about a new relationship and the prospect of living with her partner; at the same time, she can talk to her child about how he may be anything but excited and that she wouldn't be at all surprised if he were still hoping that the old family could be back together.

22

This discussion may end up being very one-sided, with the child saying little, if anything, in return, but this is one of those rare instances in which I advocate parental lectures. Sometimes it is just too confusing or threatening for children to communicate how they are feeling, and it can be far easier for a parent to guess what these feelings might be than it is for the child to express them. If you wait to hear from your daughter regarding her reaction to a stepparent's arrival you may never learn about her true feelings. Verbalizing what these feelings may be lets her know she has your concern, interest, and support, even if she does not have your enthusiasm for your future spouse. Very occasionally, parents' assumptions will be wrong, and the worst that will happen is that the child will look quizzical, roll her eyes, sigh heavily, or send another of those messages they use when they want us to know we're being boring or irrelevant, but at least she'll be aware you have been thinking about her.

Many stepparents take care to explain that they are not trying to take the place of the biological mother or father. It can take some effort and repetition, however, for children to be convinced this is so. If you are a stepparent living with the child, it may be appropriate to state clearly that you know he would prefer to have his "real" parent in the home rather than yourself. This may sound like inviting rejection, but for the child it can be important to hear that you are aware of just how special the biological parent remains in his life.

I want to return to the topic of children's play for a moment. The eagerness with which many children include both biological parents in their dream houses does not necessarily signal a wish to exclude a stepparent. It is not uncommon for children to bring both their biological and stepparents into their house and talk about their feelings of affection and love for them all. I don't doubt that the adults concerned would have some reservations about implementing such an arrangement. The message from children's play is nonetheless valuable—namely, that they can find room in their minds and affections for both biological parents and stepparents.

The loss of the nuclear family through death or divorce may always be a source of some sadness, regret, and even anger, but the more these feelings are acknowledged, understood, and expressed, the easier it is for children to allow a new parent-figure to join the list of special people in their lives.

Loss of the Single-Parent Family

Many single-parent families develop a special closeness. I lived for seven years as a single father with Joanne and Tim. We spent a great deal of time together—just the three of us. The household may have bordered on chaotic at times, but usually some semblance of order was discernible. We had our routines and rituals. If I had to go shopping, they usually came. Not that taking two small children around a grocery store and trying to explain why a cart full of marshmallows, chocolate milk, and potato chips would not encompass the four major food groups was my idea of a good time; it was just that they were too young to be left on their own and I did not have the advantage of a second parent to take care of them. They were also my company at mealtimes, and if I wanted to talk about my day, they were the audience.

For older children, being in a single-parent family can also mean assuming parts of the role that previously belonged to the spouse. A son may take on more domestic responsibilities than would otherwise be expected. A daughter may become the parent's confidant; not surprisingly, observations of family interactions tell us that children and single parents spend more time talking together than is the case in two-parent families.

In family therapy we often talk about "parental children." Sometimes this can denote a problem. For example, it can be overwhelming for a daughter if being a confidant also means she has to share the burden of the parent's worries and become the main source of emotional support. In other situations, however, having a child function as a junior parent at times can be a logical and constructive way for the family to operate. Just as occurred frequently when families tended to have large numbers of children, older siblings can share the task of caring for the younger ones. A daughter will supervise her sister until the single mother returns from work and a son will become adept at changing diapers and playing with his baby sister while supper is being prepared.

A stepparent's arrival may be seen by the children as a prime example of messing with success. They can fear that the special place and status they have enjoyed will be taken away. These fears often materialize. The parent now has a partner to share her thoughts and experiences. Domestic responsibilities may be reassigned to the stepparent and you no longer have to look for the grocery store check-out that doesn't have the candy display.

For the stepparent, the new relationship means gain; for the child, however, it can create a strong sense of loss. This is another area that often is not talked about openly in stepfamilies. Repetitious though it may be, a major part of the solution is to acknowledge, discuss, and accept the differing views and feelings that family members have. Another aspect of dealing with the loss of the single-parent family is to establish a climate in which relationships are allowed to develop and change gradually. This is a topic discussed at some length in Chapter 7.

Loss and Guilt

Parents are experts at making themselves feel guilty; it is something they seem to do naturally whenever their children are experiencing problems. Recognizing that their child is still dealing with strong feelings of loss can, therefore, provide a perfect climate for guilt to flourish. I never attempt to convince parents they have no reason to feel this way; they are often unshakeable in their view that they should give full rein to their tendency to blame themselves.

Too much guilt, however, can present a major problem for stepfamilies. A common manifestation is the "compensation package" awarded to children who are suffering from the loss of the nuclear family. It reflects a desire to at least try to make up for the fact that both parents are no longer together. "Weekend parents" may find themselves particularly susceptible to this expression of guilt. They may feel a strong wish to make the brief time they have with their children extra special. This very understandable wish, however, may become equated with providing treats and material goods to the point that the weekend becomes like Disneyland and Christmas rolled into one. A parent may also be reluctant to exert any discipline. A father who made the decision to leave the family and the home, for example, can decide he has been "mean" enough to the children, and should not, therefore, become annoyed or impose consequences when they misbehave.

Compensation packages are likely to create far more problems than they solve. The contrast between the overly indulgent and permissive parent and the one who tries to impose realistic limits can be confusing for children. It can also encourage them to play one parent against the other: accounts of how one is stingy and harsh will feed into the other's wish to be indulgent so that he can be seen as the good parent again. Children may become increasingly resistant to discipline and resentful when their demands are not met. Any stepsiblings in the family may begin to see themselves as poor relations, and this can fuel feelings of rivalry.

The most important problem with trying to assuage guilt in this way is that it falls so far short of what children want: as normal a relationship with both parents as possible. I often suggest to parents that they give thought to how a Saturday and Sunday would have been spent before the separation. It is a rare parent who has typically devoted the weekend entirely to the children. By Sunday afternoon I also expect it is a rare parent who is not finding some way to constructively ignore his children by awarding himself a time-out. Except with very young children, the pattern is likely to be one of periods together interspersed by periods spent apart. Furthermore, being together is not usually like being on vacation. I make no apology for using two clichés in a single sentence when I assert that quality time can consist of simple pleasures. We read with our children, walk to the park, make cookies, clean up the mess, derive pleasure from board games that would otherwise have us screaming with boredom, sit and watch television programs or movies, and sometimes just hang around enjoying the opportunity to be together without any particular agenda or schedule.

It would not be realistic to expect a weekend spent with a noncustodial parent to be organized in exactly the same way as might have been typical in the nuclear family. Parents who see their children for only two days out of every fourteen will often want to devote most of the access period to shared activities. But if this results in a highly organized and intense form of together-ness, the children lose the opportunity to have the more relaxed and spontaneous relationship they may have enjoyed with the parent previously. And if being special develops into being indulged, they may eventually lose the capacity to have a healthy relationship with the parent; they will begin to equate attention and affection with being "spoiled."

Although I find it difficult to talk parents out of their guilt, they can find ways to use it constructively. If a parent can be convinced that what he saw as compensation is more likely to be overindulgence and excessive permissiveness, he can begin to feel guilty about the likely impact of his actions and become motivated to implement changes. In such situations I have suggested ways for the parent and children to determine if they are resuming a normal relationship. I have asked children to keep a record of what happens during the weekend and tell them that they will know progress is being made if they see an increase in the amount of time they are bored or the number of occasions on which the parent is mad at them. I also tell the parent that a major breakthrough would be if their child exclaims in anger something to the effect, "I wish I hadn't come to see you at all." When a parent feels secure enough to exert discipline and limits and risk being unpopular, and the child feels secure enough to voice anger and displeasure, you know the relationship is back on track.

While I have used the example of weekend parents, guilt arising from children's losses can be evident in other situations. A single parent who is planning to remarry can feel she has to find a way to compensate her child, who sees only disadvantages to becoming part of a stepfamily. A stepparent who is motivated by guilt may also work far too hard at always being fair and reasonable and will deny himself the simple pleasure of uttering, "Just because I said so" when a stepchild has brought him to the brink of despair. I believe the challenge remains the same. Whenever loss is experienced, the task is to remain sensitive to how the children are feeling and, whenever possible, provide them with reassurance that, no matter what happens to the family, they are not going to lose their special place in their parents' lives. For children to be convinced, however, they must see that they can continue to rely on each parent to provide not only the obvious pleasures of life, but also the routines, guidance, and discipline that are so essential for development.

4

Writing Your Own Script

No one has managed to write a "script" for stepfamily life; as yet, there are no agreed-upon standards and procedures that can be consulted. In some respects this places stepfamilies at a disadvantage. We typically like to have a reasonably clear idea of what we should do and how we might do it. A couple with no children will have preconceived notions regarding courtship, engagement, and marriage, as will their families and friends and society at large. This script does not have to be adhered to rigidly; there is plenty of room for improvisation, but the couple is likely to retain a general understanding of how their life together will unfold. Members of stepfamilies do not have the benefit of such guidelines. What is a stepfamily *supposed* to look like, and how is it *supposed* to function? Is it a unit headed by a biological parent and stepparent together or is the stepparent more peripheral? Will old customs and habits be preserved or should they be replaced by new ones in order to strengthen the stepfamily's identity?

Specific questions like these will be returned to later; a number are also topics that will be covered in subsequent chapters. For now, however, I would like to concentrate on challenging the notion that the lack of explicit guidelines for stepfamilies is necessarily a problem. Stepfamilies vary so much in their structure and ways of operating that it would be a formidable task to write a single script for them to follow. Let's imagine, however, that you could somehow get everyone to agree on a first draft. As soon as it went to rehearsals I guarantee the complaints would be coming in fast and furious. The number of stepfamilies finding it compatible with their needs and personalities would be far outnumbered by those finding it impossible to follow. What might be helpful guidelines for one stepfamily would be unrealistic expectations for another and would cause a great deal of unnecessary aggravation.

It is true that if you don't have guidelines, the problems associated with uncertainty and ambiguity have to be faced. Just a smattering of rationalization, however, allows me to argue that uncertainty and ambiguity can result in stepfamilies enjoying a great deal of power and flexibility. Not having a readymade script means that parents and children can assume the responsibility for determining which guidelines best suit their family given their particular wishes and circumstances. I concede it is harder to write your own script, but plagiarism doesn't work too well for stepfamilies when the chances of two situations being comparable are low.

The Initial Draft

Taking the initiative for writing your own script as a stepfamily is not just a fanciful idea; it is one of proven value. Lynn Bielenberg is a social worker in Virginia who completed a research project into the effectiveness of "task-centered" group counseling with stepfamilies. Her findings illustrated the benefit of taking a preventive approach. She brought couples together in groups and presented them with a number of tasks and homework assignments, all of which were designed to increase the awareness of issues facing stepfamilies. The couples were encouraged to begin talking about the type of stepfamily they wanted to develop and how they could actively work towards this goal. The advertisements for the program led to an enthusiastic response; there was no shortage of people interested in the project. The encouraging finding was that six sessions were sufficient to bring about positive changes on some of the outcome measures. For example, the couples' level of reported stress tended to decrease and there were fewer complaints of insomnia.

Groups offer the advantage of a leader who can introduce topics and present information. They also provide the opportunity for mutual support; sometimes it is very reassuring to hear that other stepfamilies have shared your difficulties, have survived them, and may have a few ideas and suggestions for you to consider. Groups are not always accessible, however, and the alternative, do-it-yourself approach is just as valid.

The starting point I recommend is for the couple to begin discussing many different aspects of stepfamily life and reaching a tentative agreement regarding goals and expectations. This is like jointly writing the first draft. As the process develops, it may become more of a team effort in which the children are invited to become co-authors. Prior to taking this step, however, it seems to make good sense for the couple to develop an understanding of the key issues for their family and to have dealt privately with any major areas of conflict that exist between them.

There are a number of specific topics that couples may want to consider in this first draft. I have constructed a list of ten. The list is not intended to be exhaustive; it may also contain certain items that have no relevance for a particular stepfamily. Its purpose is to suggest items that might be included on the agenda.

1. Marriage: How will you ensure that you have time for each other and do not become so absorbed in the family that you forget how to be wife and husband?

2. Discipline: How extensively should the stepparent become involved in discipline? Will this involvement allow you to share responsibility with your partner or will it be a surefire way of being labeled a wicked stepparent?

3. Childcare: How involved will the stepparent be in day-to-day care of stepchildren? Do you want this to increase?

4. Affection and attachment: What steps will be taken to try to foster a bond with the stepchild? You don't have to adore one another, but can there be a midground between love and running warfare?

5. Relationship with the other biological parent: What efforts do you need to make to ensure that the stepchild does not feel her relationship with the other biological parent and extended family is being threatened or undermined by the presence of a stepparent?

6. Stepsiblings: How will stepsiblings be seen? Are they expected to become brothers and sisters or should they see themselves as friends or acquaintances?

7. Who's in the family? How involved will the stepparent's extended family be in the stepchild's life? Are a stepparent's parents the stepchild's grandparents? Does the stepchild automatically acquire an additional set of aunts, uncles, and cousins? Apart from the potential gain at Christmas and birthdays, what are the advantages to instantly creating a new branch in the family tree?

8. Naming the role: What title, or combination of titles, seems to be the best fit for the stepparent at this time? Is it acquaintance, friend, big brother, mother, uncle, polite stranger, or counselor? Is this role expected to change in the future?

9. Traditions: What should you do to preserve old customs and traditions and how can you introduce new ones so that the family can develop its own identity?
10. Quality control: How can the stage be set for regular and open discussion about family life?

Different Strokes

There are some guidelines that can be applied when discussing the above issues. For example, becoming too rapidly involved in discipline is probably not a good idea for a stepparent when the children are older. In many instances, however, there is no reason why stepfamilies should feel that one type of structure or way of operating will necessarily be better than another. Some successful stepfamilies report close relationships between stepparents and stepchildren; others do not. Some stepparents eventually become authority figures without this causing unnecessary conflict in the family; others are content to remain in the backseat.

Many factors come into play. For example, is the stepchild living in the home? Is there another biological parent and, if so, how involved is the relationship with the stepchild? How old is the stepchild? How interested are the stepparent and stepchild in having a close relationship? To some extent, factors such as these can place limits on what is realistic for the family. For example, an adolescent stepson who has a close relationship with his biological mother is likely to be less involved with a stepmother than if he were a preschooler whose biological mother had died. But within the limits that are present for a particular family, there is plenty of room for personal preferences, creativity, choice, and guesswork. The successful script is not one that conforms to any predetermined standard. Rather, it meets two criteria for the members of the stepfamily: they like it, and they feel it is one they can enact without stumbling over the lines too often.

Rewrites and Revisions

The idea that families need to periodically revise the way things are done is in no way unique to stepfamilies. For instance, a nuclear family with one child and both parents employed outside the home will undergo many changes in how it operates as it grows to the point where there are five children with one of the parents working as a full-time homemaker. Parenting styles in most families will also be modified and revamped as children leave the more dependent stages of development and approach adulthood. I nonetheless maintain that revising the script is something that needs to happen more frequently in stepfamilies than nuclear families. Stepfamilies are confronted with so many factors that are likely to have an impact on them; what is always difficult, however, is to determine exactly what the impact is going to be. I could predict that a child in a nuclear family would want more involvement in running her own life as she reaches adolescence, but I somehow doubt you would be impressed by my insight and powers of prophecy. I would be far less willing to offer an opinion as to whether or not a child is likely to become emotionally attached to a stepsibling or stepparent. My best answer would be "maybe," which would also fail to enhance my reputation as a soothsayer.

The script for stepfamilies will inevitably contain uneducated guesses and all members should reserve the right to be wrong and to change their minds accordingly.

Not Another Family Meeting

Part of the job of a family counselor is to become redundant as soon as possible. This may not be good for business, but it's ethical. One of the most effective forms of counseling is to provide family members with an approach to solving problems that they can take away and use whenever the need arises. When I have worked with stepfamilies I have often found that, after trying to convince them that their struggles and concerns are normal, my primary role is to do no more than encourage them to begin talking about their views, wishes, and feelings. Whether it is the myth of instant love, deciding which of the stepsiblings retains the job of putting out the garbage, or dealing with conflicts between custodial and noncustodial parents, most of the family members will have far more on their minds than they have expressed. When they adopt the view that family life is not supposed to follow one script and that people are not supposed to act, think, or feel in one particular way, it is easier to begin to have the type of open discussion that is necessary if problems are to be solved.

A counselor may assist in starting the process, but is not typically required for it to continue. The kitchen or living room can replace the office, and parents and children can run their own family meetings. At first this type of communication in the home can seem awkward and contrived. It may also feel threatening; who knows what others in the family think about you or how they will react when you explain your position? One way of approaching family meetings is for the parents to actively model how to listen. An atmosphere of trust and safety is much more likely to be present when people know they will be heard and believe their opinions are important. A stepmother may ask her stepson a general question about what kind of relationship he wants them to have. A mother may ask her son what he misses about the single-parent family they had previously, with the stepfather encouraging him to say whatever he wants. In so doing, the stepfather can model another essential component of this type of communication—namely, that each person's views and feelings are respected, even if they are not necessarily shared.

Regular meetings involving all members of the family may not always be appropriate. A stepmother and a stepdaughter may prefer to talk privately. They might even find it easier to put their thoughts on paper. I remember listening to a teenager talk about a letter that had been given to her by her stepfather. It was written at a time when all they seemed to do was argue. The letter mysteriously appeared behind enemy lines and, in the privacy of her room, she read about her stepfather's hope that they would find a better way of living together. She learned that, even though he was often critical of her behavior, he did see special and positive qualities in her. The Hollywood version of the story would have the stepdaughter and stepfather hugging each other and shedding tears of joy as they signed the armistice papers. It wasn't quite like that, but the letter had an impact on her that she will probably never forget.

5

Love and Marriage

The divorce rate in stepfamilies is higher than in nuclear families, but before I have you convinced that it's hopeless, I want to return to the question of how statistics are presented and interpreted. If you are in a stepfamily, you cannot escape the fact that the overall risk of divorce is higher, but there are two points that need to be made. The first is that this risk decreases after the first three years; it is the early phase of stepfamily development that seems to place particular strain on the marriage. This can offer at least some solace. If the initial problems and stresses are seen as a taste of things to come, you might feel like throwing in the towel. On the other hand, knowing that things should get better at least gives you hope on days when it seems that the only possible motivation for staying in a stepfamily is masochism.

The second point is that knowing the potential risks can be useful: it signals the need to take steps to increase the chance of not contributing to the high divorce rate. I do not pretend that there are enough data to allow me to present a recipe for a successful marriage in a stepfamily, but there are factors that appear particularly important to consider. Some relate primarily to attitudes and expectations; others are more to do with making concrete decisions and plans.

Made in Heaven? Romance and Reality

Given my love of anything with cholesterol and my allergic response to exercise, I will probably be a prime target for a heart attack at exactly that point where Kathy and I finally have time to ourselves. To me this means she won't have any noise and distraction in the house while she is nursing me back to health, but this prospect fails to impress her. When we first met on the camping trip, I had both children with me and she joined in as we celebrated Joanne's eighth birthday. After that we often double-dated—two adults, two children. We did manage the occasional candle-lit dinner on our own, but more often than not she shared the challenge of trying to get through just one meal without a drink being spilled, ketchup dripped over clean clothing, or a fight developing over who got the bigger piece of pizza.

Such is not the stuff of romance novels. We may have gazed into each other's eyes as we folded the children's laundry together, but this was not exactly what she had planned for her life.

In stepfamilies, the couple has rarely had the opportunity to devote much time to their relationship. The phase of romantic love may never have occurred and the desire to focus on one another can be overshadowed by the need to pay attention to the children. There may be no honeymoon and the luxuries of free time and privacy are often in short supply.

Rather than mourn the loss of the romantic phase, couples can take a positive view of their need to establish a working relationship, focusing on the day-to-day issues of family life. This position may be hard for me to defend, but I will present my case.

While I am all for romance, sociologists tell us that it gets people into a lot of trouble. This seems to be true for couples in all families. The more people are caught up in an idealized, romantic view of marriage, the greater tends to be their dissatisfaction as their relationship progresses. I hasten to add that it doesn't follow that the key to a successful marriage is to view it as the worst decision you have ever made and to expect it to be as exciting and rewarding as filling out a tax return. It's just that it is a rare couple that can sustain a relationship built primarily on romance.

Sociologists go on to talk about couples needing to make the transition from romantic love to conjugal love. This means that you come to terms with the fact that it is only in the world of romance movies and novels that Mr. Right never develops annoying mannerisms, a sagging waistline, and morning breath.

Conjugal love is stable. It gets you through the hard times and is characterized more by respect, understanding, and deep affection than it is by passion. Its focus is more practical than idealistic and its rewards come from a sense of accomplishment in being able to work together and support one another.

I often suggest to parents in stepfamilies that they think of themselves as essentially normal people who have simply chosen to do things backwards. Having started off their relationship with children they will have to wait awhile to enjoy a relationship as a couple. Sometimes they may not be convinced that the ten- to twenty-year waiting period will fly by, but it can be productive to begin a discussion about how a relationship based on responsibility and problem-solving can become more stable and fulfilling than one based primarily on romantic ideals. If this view can be accepted, the couple can abandon the perspective that their marriage is necessarily inferior or lacking because of the absence of a courtship phase.

I cannot leave this topic without offering some reassurance that I do not believe that couples have to resign themselves to a relationship that is all work and that any passionate thoughts or hormonal surges should be promptly suppressed. The marital relationship may not be quite the same for couples in stepfamilies as it is for those in nuclear families, but it should never be ignored.

I clearly remember watching my clinical supervisor working with a couple in a stepfamily while I was a family therapy trainee. Libby Ridgeley always went straight to the point, but her directness was matched by the concern she communicated for their relationship. Her question, "With all the time you spend looking at the children, do you ever have eyes for each other?" highlighted an issue that had been long neglected by the couple. She prescribed a remedy; one was to call the other for a date. They were to go to a restaurant on their own and the first person to talk about the children paid the bill. People rarely messed with Libby; she earned and commanded much respect, but this was a prescription the couple had a great deal of pleasure filling.

In any family, there is a risk that the demands of childrearing will overshadow the marriage. Parents can find that their relationships with the children become increasingly prominent, while their relationship with one another suffers from neglect. For stepfamilies, the lack of a courtship phase adds to the need to create opportunities to be together as a couple. Furthermore, for the stepparent who is joining a single-parent family, the quality of the marriage assumes particular significance. Single-parent families are often very close and it may take a long time before the stepparent can develop any strong attachment to the children. In all likelihood, therefore, it will be the strength of the marital relationship that will determine the extent to which the stepparent feels connected to the family.

Adjusting Your Problem Threshold

When the nuclear family has come to an end through divorce, parents can have painful memories of the problems and failures that led to the marriage breakdown. There may also have been a period prior to the separation when conflict in the home dominated day-to-day life and involved the children in one way or another. Such a background can make people particularly sensitive to any event or situation that might possibly indicate a problem in family relationships. This heightened awareness can result in relatively normal events or situations being misconstrued as a sign that there is something seriously wrong with the family.

The reaction to conflict regarding the children serves as an illustration. Studies tell us that issues concerning children are the most frequent cause of conflict between couples in stepfamilies. For some this conflict can be seen as a sign that the marriage is not working and can lead to fears of a divorce. Such fears are common; society is reasonably tolerant of one divorce, but a second failed marriage can cause others to wonder if there is something wrong with the person. The parent, of course, may also entertain similar self-doubts.

But how abnormal is it for couples to find that children place strain on the marriage? The answer is that, in nuclear families, having a child decreases marital satisfaction. This is not proof positive that children are dangerous to your health, but it does illustrate that, however welcomed and loved the new member of the family may be to her biological parents, she takes some getting used to. There may be differing expectations regarding the definition of roles and conflict regarding the distribution of tasks in the family; roughly translated, this means there may be heated debates about who gets up in the middle of the night and whether or not one gender is more innately qualified to change diapers than the other. If it is the first baby, parents can also be feeling anxious about their child-rearing skills, as well as learning the hard way just how tiring it can be to care for an infant.

It seems, therefore, that stepparents are far from alone in finding that the children place strain on the marriage. They will also be in good company if they are having more than the odd skirmish with any adolescents in the family. The research tells us that teenagers have most of their arguments with family members. It can be easier for parents in nuclear families to treat this type of conflict as part of a normal phase, even though it can be stressful and wearing at times. The same conflict between a stepparent and teenage stepchild, however, can too readily be interpreted as a sign that the stepfamily is failing.

The fact that a problem is common to parents in all types of families does not, of course, make it go away, but it does offer a small measure of comfort. Whether it is stress regarding how to deal with children, making the transition from a largely single social life to forging friendships with other families, or reaching an agreement regarding financial matters, couples in stepfamilies can expect to find the adjustment to family life complex and demanding at times. Recognizing that this is normal, however, can help couples tackle problems as they arise rather than seeing them as signs of impending doom.

Who's in Charge?

From my contact with stepfamilies it often seems as if there is a lack of clarity regarding how decisions should be made. I sometimes ask the family members to explain exactly who holds the power when it comes to certain decisions. Are issues decided jointly or by one person more than the other? Are people content with this arrangement or are there matters over which the husband or wife is trying to claim jurisdiction?

The question of power can lead to conflict in any marriage, but it frequently seems to be a major issue in stepfamilies and one, therefore, that needs to be addressed openly. Couples can be well-advised to discuss their expectations regarding how much control each will have individually and how much decision-making will be shared.

Of all the issues in my own stepfamily, those relating to power and control have probably surfaced most frequently. I know I have an attitude problem when it comes to authority; I was told this in school and it was one of the few times in my rebellious youth that I found my teachers to be credible. Kathy, on the other hand, wholeheartedly believes in the concept of authority, as long as she has it. So our getting married was seen by those who knew us well as more reminiscent of *Clash of the Titans* than *Love Story*. In addition to our personality styles, I had a history of seven years as a single parent. I had made the decisions and I had supported the family financially. I had run the whole show and I had taken full responsibility for what happened. Making the transition from "I" to "we" was not easy.

Many single parents find themselves in a similar position. Given that most are women, gender roles and stereotypes can be very relevant. Whatever disadvantages and stresses may be associated with the role, a number of single mothers find it allows them to gain a certain self-confidence and independence that they may not have experienced previously. This is particularly likely to be true if the first marriage was highly traditional and stereotyped, with the husband occupying the position of head of the family. Separation can lead to a resumption of a career that was put on hold and to the need to take charge of family finances. A woman discovers she is more than equipped to manage a career and family, and can do all this successfully without a partner. The realization that a man is more a habit or luxury than a necessity can generate the concern that remarriage will entail loss of status and independence.

Although the results from the research are not always consistent, it has been found that remarried women have greater power than in their first marriages. For men, the opposite trend can hold true. The net effect is that an egalitarian style of management and control is common in many, although not all areas of decision-making. Counseling groups preparing couples for remarriage will often have this issue high on the agenda for discussion. Much negotiation, understanding, and sensitivity can be necessary between the couple before a relationship can be established in which both can feel powerful while neither feels dominated.

I made reference to the likelihood that power will not be shared in all areas. Single mothers entering a stepfamily typically retain the deciding, and sometimes only vote on child-related matters. In many respects this can be an example of when it is preferable not to share power equally. Problems are often created when a stepparent, either by invitation or insistence, moves too rapidly in asserting authority over the stepchildren. Older children and adolescents are particularly likely to see such a stepparent as an intruder whose efforts to assume a parental role will be resisted and resented. Over time, the balance of power may shift, but it may be wise for the couple to acknowledge that one of them will be number-one parent and that any transition to a more egalitarian style will be made only gradually.

I must leave plenty of room for exceptions. Some marriages work very well with one person as the dominant partner in the relationship. Mine would if we could only agree who should get the top job. Certain factors may also influence decision-making regarding children. If the stepchildren are young and the other biological parent is absent or minimally involved, it may be both feasible and desirable for the stepparent to quickly assume responsibility for child-rearing. What is worthwhile in all instances, however, is for the couple to take the time to reach an understanding of how power will be held and exercised in their marriage and family life.

Financial Management

Financial matters are one of the most frequent areas of difficulty reported by couples in stepfamilies. It is nonetheless ironic that I find myself actually publishing an opinion regarding anything to do with money. Financial management is not a personal forte. As Kathy delights in recalling, it is no exaggeration that, when I was a single parent, I used the fruit-basket system of bill-paying. In case you're not familiar with this system, it entails putting all the bills in a basket. When you get your paycheck you close your eyes and pull out that week's lucky winner. The rest can wait and take their chances next week. For reasons that should now be obvious, Kathy viewed establishing a joint account after we married with considerable trepidation. There is some evidence, however, that foolhardy though this decision may have seemed at the time, it was probably a good move.

Marilyn Coleman and Lawrence Ganong at the University of Missouri have been actively involved in stepfamily research for many years. They devoted one study to an investigation of financial management practices among remarried couples with children. Their data suggested that, in keeping with the discussion in the previous section, women tended to have more say regarding financial matters in stepfamilies than in their first marriages. Overall, the most common style of financial management was egalitarian, with income and other resources being pooled. A relationship between financial management practices and closeness in the family was also documented. Specifically, families in which resources were pooled reported greater closeness between stepparents and stepchildren. As Coleman and Ganong are quick to point out, the finding that two things are related does not necessarily mean one causes the other; you cannot assume that relationships will become closer just by pooling finances. The reason for the association between these factors is not clear. It is possible that the degree of commitment to the new family is the critical link; this factor could have an impact on both the closeness of relationships and the willingness to share resources.

Differences between stepfamilies need to be considered as complex financial arrangements regarding support payments and shared costs of custodial children may make it expedient to maintain at least some separation between the husband's and wife's assets and incomes. For those parents and stepfamilies who come to see me and, because of lack of awareness of my personal history, request an opinion regarding finances, I nonetheless suggest that they start with the notion of pooling their resources and then proceed to discuss any reasons why it would be preferable to keep certain financial aspects separate. I take care never to assume that one partner necessarily wants the other to share expenses. Custodial mothers, for example, sometimes report ambivalent feelings regarding the stepfather's contributing to childcare costs. On the one hand, it can be seen as a sign of their husband's interest and commitment; on the other, the mother can feel it is an unfair burden on her spouse, particularly if he has financial obligations to help support children from a previous marriage. How each person feels about a particular financial arrangement will, therefore, need to be weighed by the couple just as heavily as how practical it may be at the moment or how beneficial it could prove to be in the long-term. As always, almost any arrangement can work and individual needs and circumstances should not be overshadowed by overall trends. Above all, I recommend that this area is given some prominence on the list of topics to be considered in the marriage.

Family and Friends

Just as couples can have less time for one another than they would like, the demands of stepfamily life can result in their neglecting their relationships with friends and extended family. It could be argued that this is a necessary change; perhaps it is important for the couple to establish the boundaries around themselves and concentrate on investing their time and energy in the new family. There is probably truth to this argument, but it also emerges that becoming too insular can entail costs. In a study of marital relationships in stepfamilies, it was found that one factor predicting adjustment was the nature of the relationship with extended family and friends. Couples reporting a higher quality of such relationships were more likely to report a higher quality of marital adjustment.

As I was reading this study I was reminded of how often I have met parents who seem to have almost no life outside their work and stepfamilies. It is not that they have no interest in other areas; it's just that they feel they have no time to devote to outside relationships and activities. The "trickle-down" theory needs to be introduced here. This is the idea that when adults in a family are in good shape it helps everything else fall into place; the parents' contentment trickles down to their offspring. The theory has been very popular in family therapy, but it doesn't seem to hold up very well for stepfamilies. It appears that stepparents can have a wonderful marriage, but this has little to do with the quality of the relationship with a stepchild. Such a relationship has to be worked on directly. I suspect that parents in stepfamilies intuitively know the fallacy of the trickle-down theory and decide that their needs as individuals and as a couple have to be shelved while they concentrate on their children. As a result, their social life can become extinct in the same way that their identity as a couple can fail to receive the attention it deserves.

I have had to encourage couples to learn how to be self-centered. It's a dying art and one I want to be remembered for as reviving in stepfamilies. My justification is simply that all members of stepfamilies are important and deserve attention. The laws of nature may require that we give precedence to children and I can see that, if there is a shortage of space in the lifeboat, it is the parents who are out of luck. But in the absence of such dire straits, parents can claim the right to think of themselves on occasion.

Focusing on the stepfamily needs to be balanced by maintaining and developing an active social support system. That's how sociologists describe the importance of getting away from it all, having a shoulder to cry on, and people with whom you can share your achievements, goals, and fantasies. For me it means trying to convince Kathy that my wish to spend a week canoeing with friends is no more than a reflection of my desire to strengthen our relationship. She's sceptical, but I did manage to get away for four days last year.

6

Discipline

You Can't Tell Me What to Do

Sooner or later most stepparents will be reminded that they are not really a parent. Not that stepparents are unaware of this fact; it's just that stepchildren like to keep this piece of information as a trump card to be played at opportune moments. The standard form is, "You're not my mother, you can't tell me what to do"; rarely do you hear, "You're not my mother, you can't drive me to the mall," or "I don't have to eat these home-baked chocolate chip cookies, you're not my father."

An important question to be resolved in the family is the

extent to which a stepparent should become involved in discipline. In reaching this decision, it can be helpful to think about how the two primary roles of parents evolve; these roles are nurturing and guidance. An essential part of the latter role is exercising discipline. In nuclear families parents readily combine the two roles. The parent who hugs her daughter when she returns from school may scold her on discovering that yet another glove has been donated to the lost and found box. A teenager may look for reassurance from a parent regarding how he looks before going out to a dance, only to be grounded the same evening for ignoring his curfew.

Because biological parents typically have the responsibility for both nurturing and discipline, stepparents can often feel they are supposed to follow suit. In some stepfamilies, this can become a guaranteed way of creating conflict, particularly if the stepchildren are adolescents. Historically, however, parents in nuclear families do not immediately assume both roles for the simple reason that there is almost no need to discipline infants. With very few exceptions, a baby's behavior is accepted for what it is. The mother obviously does not establish limits regarding how many diaper changes are permissible or impose consequences for crying or waking up in the night. The baby's extreme dependency and helplessness permit the parent to have a great deal of control. It is only when the infant gets older and begins to have choices regarding what she will do that the question of who will be in charge is opened up for debate. So the first year or so can be almost exclusively a period of nurturing. It is a time when the infant is fed, cuddled, rocked, bathed, and sung to, as well as all those other wonderful things that help the emotional bond become strong and secure.

The child's acceptance of the parent's right to guide and discipline follows this period of attachment. Children develop a desire to please the people who have become the most important figures in their lives and who have a proven track record when it comes to providing physical and emotional care. This desire to please may, of course, seem well and truly hidden at times, but even during the most heated arguments and disagreements in nuclear families, the underlying wish to have the approval of the parent is almost certainly there.

In most situations, the stepparent is entering a family in which a system of discipline has already been established. Typically, however, the stepparent has not had the opportunity to form the type of attachment with the child that develops through nurturing. The question to be decided is how much involvement there should be in matters of discipline. This will apply just as much when stepchildren are living with the other biological parent and visit periodically. No matter how much time the children are in the home, there will need to be an understanding regarding who sets the rules and who will enforce them.

A starting point is to consider the merits of the stepparent having as little direct responsibility for discipline as possible. The Fosters were a stepfamily I became quite attached to, but preferred to see fairly late in the evening to avoid disturbing other people in the building. Abby was one of those preadolescent girls I would love to have as a grandchild; her energy, humor, warmth, and self-confidence would endear her to me between two and five on a Sunday afternoon, but her belief that the age of majority should be lowered to twelve would make her a challenge to parent. The concerns expressed in the family were mainly behavioral; it wasn't that Abby was seen as a bad child, she was just very difficult and argumentative. Her mother would give an example of a conflict; almost immediately this would be reenacted with Abby providing a loud and contradictory version of what had happened. As the stepfather moved in to support his wife, however, the topic would be changed rapidly to that of whether or not he was entitled to have any say in what she did. Abby had a seemingly endless number of variations of the "You're not my father" line and each one prompted a renewed, but ineffective attempt on the stepfather's part to assert his authority. As daughter and stepfather locked horns yet again, the rest of the family and I became the audience.

We scheduled a cabinet meeting—just the parents, Jim and Debbie, and myself. I am particular about how these are orchestrated. The whole family was invited, but I asked the parents to instruct Abby and her younger brother to stay in the waiting room while we had a meeting. Some family therapists call this "boundary making"; it's a way of reinforcing the idea that sometimes parents have to make decisions that are passed down to the children. I like it because it drives the kids crazy not knowing what we are up to; a well-placed measure of anxiety can be a great therapeutic tool. Behind closed doors we talked about possible ways of changing the organization in the family. Debbie and Jim brought up the issue of the right to discipline. I have no argument with the position that, as an adult in the family, a stepparent has the right to more power and influence than the children. But, while Jim had the right to assume a disciplinary role, he also had the right to a long life and happiness. The former was in jeopardy and the latter was clearly being violated. He was unable to give any other example of a job he had accepted that offered no pleasure, no pay, and no hope of advancement. While I felt it premature to ask him to resign, I suggested that he and Debbie think about a temporary leave of absence.

The recommendation to parents that they do less or nothing is always the hardest to make. When families are struggling with a problem, they want to actively work toward a solution. What helped Jim and Debbie decide to accept the recommendation, however, was their awareness that the battles over who had the right to discipline were getting them nowhere, as well as making it almost impossible for Jim to enjoy the time he spent with Abby. The conflicts also obscured issues that needed to be dealt with in the family. Instead of the much-needed negotiation regarding what rules, incentives, and consequences should be in place, they were stuck on the question of who should be at the bargaining table.

A new position for Jim was established. He was hired primarily as Debbie's consultant. She would have the final say, but would ask his opinion at times, just as he would offer his whenever he felt so inclined. It was Debbie, however, who would deal directly with Abby on all matters concerning discipline whenever possible. If problems arose when Debbie was not present, Jim would remind Abby of what her mother would expect her to do. If necessary, he would tell her that he would be letting her mother know if she decided to ignore the rules. He would only move in to take over control in dire emergencies; otherwise, Abby was answerable to her mother.

The understanding that, although Debbie was responsible for discipline, Jim would voice his opinions at times allowed him to have a measure of indirect power. The expectation that a stepparent will only speak when spoken to can create its own set of problems; it can be very stressful to live with children who have habits and behaviors you feel should be added to the criminal code. It would be most unusual for a parent and stepparent to start with the same standards for children's behavior, and regular cabinet meetings may be necessary to effect a compromise between the existing regime and the stepparent's views and wishes. Ideally, however, any changes that are decided upon will be implemented gradually; resentment is likely to be fostered if the stepparent is seen as the one who makes the rules, even though he may not be the enforcer.

Back to Abby, who was ushered into the cabinet room, obviously wanting to know what we'd been plotting, but doing her best to feign complete indifference. We went through formal introductions, whereby each member of the family was given a job description. Her mother explained her position, including her role as the authority figure; Jim explained his. I added that Abby's task was to find another technique for diverting attention away from her behavior. Without any opposition to the "You're not my father" statement, she was defenseless. I'm sure she worked hard to find one, but once diversionary tactics have been labeled as such in a family, they tend to lose their effectiveness.

Sometimes family therapy can seem manipulative. The intention, however, is to enact what needs to happen in the family. Excluding children from discussions often has the goal of helping them become closer to parents. Over time, Abby began to change her view of her stepfather as a sparring partner. This allowed her to develop healthier ways of relating to him and it was obviously a source of much pleasure for them both to find they could actually enjoy one another's company on occasion.

When comparisons have been made of stepfamilies who feel they have been successful and those who do not, significant differences have been found in the extent of the stepparent's involvement in discipline and other aspects of decision-making that relate to the stepchildren. By and large, success is associated with either minimal involvement or a very gradual increase in assuming these types of responsibilities. If a stepparent is not bringing children into the home, this lack of involvement can seem unfair. After all, marriage is supposed to involve sharing, and if your spouse has single-handedly coped with the daily demands and stresses of child-rearing, shouldn't you be willing to help out? While this logic cannot be faulted, the advantages of sharing a task can quickly vanish if the net result is a level of tension and conflict in the home that is taking the joy out of family life.

Another concern can be that lack of involvement in discipline will maintain the stepparent's peripheral role and make it harder for him to become a full member of the family. The opposite is probably true in most situations. Acceptance and attachment are more likely to develop when emphasis is placed on allowing the stepparent and children to gradually get to know one another. Just as instant love is an unrealistic expectation, so is instant respect as an authority figure. Assuming this role too quickly can create a level of conflict and resentment that impedes rather than fosters the relationship between the stepparent and stepchild.

I have to return to the principle that there is no one script that is applicable to all stepfamilies. Situations will exist in which it is very difficult for the stepparent to avoid taking an active role in discipline. The biological parent may be absent from the home because of shift work or the need to travel on business, and the stepparent will be left to manage the household on a regular basis. It is nonetheless possible for the biological parent to retain much of the responsibility for establishing the rules. The family can sit together to discuss matters relating to discipline and children can be made aware that, although the stepparent has an influence on the decisions that are made, they are, above all, accountable to their biological parent. A parallel in the workforce is the expectation that when the boss is absent, she will delegate someone to be in charge. This person may need to interpret the policies and procedures, but will not change them or establish new ones.

Issues concerning discipline can become more complicated when both parents bring children into the stepfamily. I would still advocate the same starting point: one parent disciplines his children, while the other disciplines hers. In this situation, however, changes may need to occur more rapidly than in a stepfamily in which only one parent has children. It would be unusual to find two parents who have exactly the same attitudes towards childrearing. Although the research has yet to be conducted, I am confident that if you asked two single parents why they had fallen madly in love, sharing the same ideas regarding how children should behave at the meal table or how much allowance they should receive would not be high on the list of reasons. If the parenting styles and expectations are close, family life can proceed with the children being answerable primarily to their respective biological parents. Tension and dissatisfaction can arise, however, if the differences between the parenting styles are pronounced. A thirteen-year-old boy may have had no difficulty accepting a ten o'clock bedtime, but will be incited to mutiny on learning that his twelve-year-old stepsister can decide when to go to bed. Similarly, having the task of doing the dishes regularly will no longer be seen as fair if it seems that your stepbrother's only job is to dirty them.

The more the two parents differ in their approaches and expectations, the more likely it is that one will be seen as unjust and too strict. This can create a great deal of conflict and the decision may be made to move towards a middle ground so there can be more consistency with respect to discipline. This requires embarking on a process of negotiation and compromise in which both parents should have equal power and in which neither approach is assumed to be superior to the other. If one parent is perceived as the victor because of successfully asserting his practices and beliefs, he can become a ready target for his stepchildren's resentment of the "takeover." Open discussion in which the children participate and hear the parents express mutual respect and reach joint decisions can make it far easier for all members of the family to accept changes in how the home is to be structured and managed. The principle that each child is answerable to his or her biological parent can remain. As in any stepfamily, this may change over time, but it may not. A stepparent's gradual assumption of equal responsibility for discipline is best seen as a possibility, not a requirement.

7

Love, Care, and Affection

Do I Have to Like You?

One of the biggest unknowns for stepfamilies is the extent to which emotional attachments will form. The norm for nuclear families is for a strong bond to be present between children and parents; there is no such norm for stepfamilies.

I like to suggest that parents take the time to discuss what kind of relationships they hope will develop and compare this to the type of relationship they feel will be realistic. Often these are not the same, but once this is acknowledged, a compromise position can be sought. At the extreme, the issue may be straightforward. If the stepchild is very young, lives in the home, and either has lost the biological parent through death or has very little contact with that parent, it may be a natural process for a strong emotional attachment to develop that both want and enjoy without reservation. The other extreme can be a stepfamily in which the child is, in fact, almost an adult and is getting ready to leave home. While uncertainty and perhaps conflict regarding the relationship may arise, the nurturing role will not be one that the stepparent has the opportunity to consider or develop in any large measure.

In between these extremes, the possibilities are endless. Factors such as how much time the stepchildren are in the home and the strength of the attachment to the same-sex biological parent have to be considered. Then there is the age of the child. A boy who is entering simultaneously his adolescence and a stepfamily can be faced with two opposing forces. An essential part of adolescence is preparing to move away from the family; this maturational process provides young people with the drive to become independent and their parents with the hope of peace in their old age. But if the stepson is expected to develop an increasingly close relationship with the stepfather, he is confronted with the task of moving closer and moving away at the same time. The conflict that is created can be intense and hard to resolve. For a five-year-old stepdaughter, on the other hand, the expectation that a fairly close relationship will develop over time can often prove realistic.

The child's personality is another important factor. Some children warm to adults quickly, are naturally outgoing, and accept or even welcome change. Others are less inclined to let new people into their lives, preferring to meet their needs through tried and true relationships. Consequently, one child may be far more receptive to a relationship with a stepparent than another of identical age and similar family history. This situation can increase in complexity when there is more than one stepchild. As any parent with two or more children can attest, siblings who have the same biological parents and the same home environment can be like night and day when it comes to their personalities. Such differences can be strong and can override the effects of age; as a result, an older stepchild may develop an attachment to the stepparent more readily than a younger sibling.

While on the topic of personality, I want to raise an issue that sometimes seems to be taboo in stepfamilies. We tend to assume that parents like their children; for stepfamilies, however, this is another one of those assumptions that cannot be applied automatically. In nuclear families the period of early attachment and bonding almost guarantees that the biological parents will have a warm and positive view of the children; this may be masked by the aggravation that goes along with being a parent at times, but it is rarely eroded. Most stepparents, however, are introduced to a child who is both a stranger and who already has a distinct personality. The idea that you should automatically like this child is as questionable as the idea that you should automatically like anyone, large or small, that you meet in the course of your daily life. Just as a stepchild may not warm to a stepparent, a stepparent's reaction to the child may be one of indifference or even dislike.

The presence of a taboo regarding this topic was a major obstacle for a stepfamily I worked with many years ago. I remember Karen as a parent who took great pleasure in devoting much of her time to her two preadolescent daughters, Kim and Jessie. There was no doubt she had more than earned the right to be proud of how well they were doing, particularly as she had shouldered almost all of the responsibility for raising them since the separation. Her new partner, Rob, had been in the family for just over a year, and although he seemed to get along with Kim, Karen expressed much disappointment that his relationship with Jessie did not appear to be developing. She complained that he avoided Jessie and that any contact between them was never more than superficial.

As I spent time with the family, it became obvious that Rob liked Kim far more than her sister. He always looked at her when she spoke in sessions and she often smiled when he did so. He laughed at her jokes and I could easily sense his enthusiasm when he talked about activities they had shared. His reaction to Jessie, however, was more one of indifference. They were sitting in the same room together, but that was about all they appeared to have in common.

It took several sessions before Rob would express how he felt about Jessie. He knew how proud Karen was of both girls. It was not that she thought they were perfect. She recognized their faults and worked to correct them, but saw these as only minor flaws. In her eyes, Kim and Jessie were wonderful children. For a long time, however, Rob had doubted he could ever share this view of Jessie. He found her ingratiating at times, thought she was too bossy with her friends, and generally felt they had little in common.

Telling a parent you don't think her child is wonderful is not an easy matter, although it is hardly a rare experience to entertain such a thought. If you made a list of all the children you come into contact with regularly, chances are there would be several that evoke no more than neutral feelings and at least one or two you don't particularly like. To voice such opinions, however, would normally serve no purpose except to upset the parents unnecessarily. It would also jeopardize friendships; I'm not sure how kindly I would take to someone saying, "Peter, I like you, but your children fill me with indifference."

Being no exception, Rob had kept his feelings and opinions to himself. Discussion with the couple alone was directed towards the rules that seemed to be operating in the family. Did Rob *have* to see the girls in the same way as Karen? Did he *have* to see Jessie and Kim in the same way? It usually happens that, once parents begin talking about the unwritten and unspoken rules that may have been operating, they either begin to allow for exceptions or abandon them entirely. The more Karen acknowledged that Rob's reaction to the children would be different from hers and would be more strongly influenced by the degree of match between their personalities than is true for biological parents, the more Rob admitted it was no mystery to him why he and Jessie were somewhat distant. Eventually this became a topic the whole family felt comfortable discussing. It was a relief to abandon the idea that everything had to be equal. Rob was almost certainly going to become a father-figure for Kim. For Jessie he was currently little more than her mother's partner; when asked what he wanted to become, he replied, "Someone she can trust and respect." Jessie set a similar goal for herself.

One reason for talking about the family is that I met Kim and Jessie recently. They are young adults and live together in their own apartment. They began telling me about their teen years. What I found interesting was that Jessie and Rob had worked out a relationship that suited them both well. They had not become particularly close, but had become accustomed to living with one another. It was much like a number of relationships people have with fellow employees. She commented that she knew their relationship had improved when she reached the point where she found herself wanting to buy him a birthday present instead of doing so just to please her mother.

Kim's relationship with Rob has been far less predictable. It seemed that, as Rob had become very involved as a parent, he was inevitably part of dealing with the issues of control and the struggles for independence that can mark the teenage years. Kim readily accepted his role as someone who provided care, but she recalled having mixed feelings when it came to his being an authority figure. There were a number of very heated "You're not my father" arguments and there was a time when their relationship was anything but cordial and civil.

It can be hard to know at the outset what type of relationship will develop between stepparents and stepchildren. Our own stepfamily also illustrates the range of outcomes. Writing this book motivated me to ask Joanne and Tim about how they see their relationship with Kathy after knowing her for over half their lives. I was interested in the label each would use to describe her role. Joanne initially said "friend," but almost immediately added that this was insufficient. She eventually settled for "special friend." Tim offered "90 percent mother," with 10 percent undecided.

The point I want to emphasize is that it is helpful to be open to a broad range of possibilities. A stepfather may never expect to be close to his stepchild or he may see himself taking the role of an older friend, uncle, big brother, or father. In some instances a stepparent may want to adopt a stepchild, although this tends to be uncommon when there is a noncustodial parent present. It can become an option, however, in situations where the child had lost a parent through death or the noncustodial parent has very little involvement or interest in the child's life. The nature of the relationship is an area of stepfamily life that often needs to be discussed and negotiated. What tends to create frustration and disappointment is when one person's view of what the relationship is supposed to be is very different from the other's.

Many stepparents will state explicitly that they are not trying to take the place of the same-sex biological parent. This will ideally be followed by discussing what type of role the stepparent will have. Inviting suggestions from stepchildren may sound risky; there is always a chance they will suggest "long- and still-lost cousin" or "penpal," but take the risk. If the only option that emerges is "polite stranger," then this can be the starting point. It may not seem like much, but it characterizes how we relate to many people we encounter, and it's far better than "arch enemy."

Taking It Slow

Whenever possible, I suggest that stepfamilies create the expectation that the relationship between stepparents and stepchildren will be allowed to develop slowly. Put another way, you can try to speed things up, but you can't escape the fact that when people in a relationship want to move at different speeds, it's the slower one who sets the pace. Recognizing this leads many stepparents to adopt the view that they should allow their stepchildren to come to them. It can be very difficult to know when a stepchild is ready to move closer to you emotionally, but the likelihood that this will occur is increased when he knows that such movement would be welcomed, but is not demanded or necessarily anticipated.

It can be helpful to think in terms of years rather than months. Even for young children, one study found that it took up to two years before a number of stepfathers felt they had a comfortable relationship with their stepchildren. If the stepchildren are older, it may well take much longer; estimates of five years are not unusual when people write about the process of establishing a solid relationship with adolescent stepchildren.

Provided the stepparent has some involvement in childcare, the early phase of the relationship can be viewed as similar to the beginning of a friendship. An obvious part of friendship is being willing to do things for the other person. In any family there is no shortage of tasks to be taken on, ranging from cooking meals and helping with school projects, to providing taxi services and repairing toys. Another part of friendship is enjoying time together. This may be more challenging; it can be much easier to find something to do *for* stepchildren than something to do *with* them. Remembering that there are many degrees of togetherness can be helpful. Watching a stepson's basketball game may not exactly be intimate, but at least the two of you are in the same place and sharing the experience. At some point you may enjoy sitting together to watch a game on television and move on to taking practice shots against each other in the driveway, but all in good time.

Stepparents can become frustrated when the relationship seems to be moving at a slow pace, or perhaps not moving at all. At such times there can be some comfort to be had from the research. Stepfamilies who pass tests of adjustment and global satisfaction with flying colors tend to report two things. The first is that emotional attachments have developed slowly; presumably they allow the pace to be leisurely so that the stepchildren are less likely to get anxious or threatened from feeling that the stepparent was trying to move into their lives too quickly. The second is that success was not necessarily associated with having close relationships; it seems there are a number of stepfamilies that reach the stage where they see themselves as secure and well-adjusted and in which stepparents and stepchildren are more than content to view themselves as acquaintances or casual friends.

A relationship that feels stuck may denote a problem, but it can also be the case that the relationship has reached the level of its potential, at least for the time being. Enjoying it for what it is will be far more profitable than lamenting what it has not, and perhaps can never become.

One-way Streets

Parallels between a friendship and a steprelationship exist, but there are also noticeable differences. Friendships are usually reciprocal; we expect that our interest in the other person will be met with similar enthusiasm. If I find that I am the only one who calls the other person or suggests we get together, I will eventually come to the realization that he finds my company less than stimulating. I can then look elsewhere to try to cultivate friendships. Stepparents are not in this position. They cannot trade in their stepchildren if their overtures of interest, affection, and friendship are met with yawns, derisive laughter, or a turned back.

Sam and Regina Vuchinich at Oregon State University and their colleagues observed videotapes of twenty-six stepfamilies in which there were early adolescent children. Each family was taped while they were eating supper. They not only did this once, they returned two years later to have another look. Their interest was in evaluating how members of stepfamilies interact—particularly stepfathers and their stepchildren.

It could be argued that having a video camera pointed at the table would not only stop people from eating their chicken with their fingers, but would also ensure that a façade of politeness is maintained, even when a food fight was the norm. This rarely seems to happen, however; inhibitions are usually temporary and chances are good that the behavior observed will be representative of family life.

The researchers rated the videotapes in a number of ways. For example, they noted prosocial behavior such as compliments, oppositional behavior such as disagreements and insults, and commands, questions, and answers. Interactions could then be coded. A stepfather's, "How do you like my casserole?" followed by his stepdaughter's "I hope they bury the recipe with you—tomorrow," would be coded question-answer/opposition.

I want to mention just a few of the results. They noted that stepfathers seemed to be making a "sustained effort to develop better relationships with their stepchildren" over the two-year period. Their adolescent children, on the other hand, seemed to be making a sustained effort to ignore these overtures. This was especially true for the girls. It wasn't that the stepchildren were typically out-and-out obnoxious; they just tended to ignore their stepfathers or responded to them with barely a flicker of life.

What amazed me was that the stepfathers were still plugging away with questions like "Did you have a good day at school?"

and "How's your dinner?" Presumably they had adopted a view that a grunt in return would be a major breakthrough. I should add that biological parents may be no strangers to this type of one-way street with their adolescents; it seems, however, that stepparents are more likely to find themselves in this position.

I offer no ready solution. In general, part of being a stepparent is often to invest a lot more than you feel is ever returned. To some extent, stepparents have to live with this inequity and imbalance and many find they need particularly thick skins if they are to survive without reacting too personally to their daily ration of rejection. On a more optimistic note, they may eventually see more of a return than anticipated. The extent of the child's appreciation for the stepparent may not emerge until later; possibly not until adulthood. While still growing up, there may be too much in the way—for example, confusion regarding allegiances to the stepparents and biological parents, reluctance to move too close to the stepparent because of fears he too may leave, or concentrating on belonging to a peer group rather than forming new family ties. Avoiding chronic frustration requires a willingness to adjust the goals for the relationship so that expectations are not too discrepant from those of the stepchild. As well as accepting that progress will be slow, goals should be modest and the investment long-term.

Although less common, lack of reciprocity in a relationship can also result from the stepchild's wanting more than the stepparent is prepared to give. A girl may truly want her stepfather to be a warm, nurturing, and affectionate parent, but the stepfather may not experience this type of emotional attachment to her. This can be a hard situation to resolve because of the fears parents have about hurting children's feelings, particularly children who may still be dealing with the losses associated with separation or death. Ignoring the imbalance, however, is rarely satisfactory. Most children are very perceptive when it comes to gauging how adults feel about them, and when the situation is not dealt with openly, they can end up feeling hurt, angry, and rejected.

Some of the hardest sessions I have had with stepfamilies were when a stepparent has decided to explain the limits of the relationship he can have with a stepchild. What can make it easy is to spend much of the time talking about those aspects of the relationship that are realistic, as opposed to those that are not. Being told that her friendship is important and being reminded of the ways in which her company is enjoyed can help a stepdaughter realize that although the relationship may never meet her hopes, it is something to be proud of and foster. The closest parallel I can think of is, "I don't want to go out with you, but I'd like to keep you as a friend." It was certainly a proposal I heard frequently in my youth, and while my fantasies may have been crushed, my ego recovered and I even gained a few special and lasting friendships.

Affection and Sexuality

Physical affection is often an accepted and unquestioned part of life in a nuclear family. We hold, stroke, kiss, and rub noses with infants. While most older children would draw the line at nose-rubbing, they will usually continue to display affection physically. A father can hug his teenage daughter and a mother can kiss her adolescent son, although perhaps with a limit of twice a week and never in public. The innocence of such physical expression is rarely questioned. Although we have become increasingly aware of sexual abuse in families, it remains true that, in the vast majority of relationships between parents and their biological children, the distinction between affection and sexuality does not become blurred.

Developmentally, the "incest taboo" is probably reinforced by the parent's early involvement in childcare. There is research suggesting that taking part in the daily physical care of infants is one reason why parents do not subsequently see their children in a sexual light. Parents routinely undress small children, bathe them or even bathe with them, and cuddle next to them in bed. This physical intimacy remains uncomplicated and innocent; the need to maintain a boundary between affection and sexuality seldom becomes an issue. Stepparents may not have this history of providing care for their stepchildren. The absence of a period in which physical affection has become a natural and accepted part of their relationship can place them in an awkward position, particularly with adolescent stepchildren. A stepfather may want to hug his teenage stepdaughter, but may feel uncomfortable doing so. He may be concerned about how she will interpret his actions; he may also be particularly ambivalent about hugging her if he sees her as physically attractive.

Addressing the question of attractiveness first, there is no reason why stepparents need to feel strange or "weird" if they become aware of the physical characteristics of a stepson or stepdaughter. Biological parents and adults in general have definite opinions regarding such matters. No one would consider it abnormal to hear a parent, uncle, or grandmother commenting on how pretty or handsome a child looked. Furthermore, they would not be considered off-base if a comment were made regarding how a child's appearance might add to the need to establish guidelines regarding dating before grade seven.

Being aware of your opinions regarding a stepchild's physical attractiveness is as unavoidable as it is normal. It is only if this awareness dominates the perception of the stepchild and develops into a sexual attraction that a problem exists that should be addressed with a counselor or therapist.

The question remains as to whether or not stepparents should actually be physically affectionate towards their stepchildren. Will "maybe" do as an answer? Families, and individuals within them, vary a great deal with respect to how physically demonstrative they prefer to be. All I suggest to stepparents is that they try operating primarily on instinct and emotion. If a stepfather wants to put his arm around his stepson's shoulders or sit next to his stepdaughter when watching television, he should do so. If the child moves away or quickly relocates to another seat, view it as one of life's minor, but inevitable rejections. The best course of action at that point would probably be to accept that affection will have to be expressed in other ways. This may eventually change, but it may not. Either way, it is usually wise to accept the stepchild's wish for distance and allow him to take the initiative for any physical affection that occurs in the future.

Problems can also develop when older stepchildren are physically attracted to a stepparent. A stepparent may be closer in age to the stepchild than the biological parent and it would not be abnormal, for example, for a teenage boy to find a woman in her twenties attractive. Adolescents can also develop crushes and can begin fantasizing about a romantic relationship with a stepparent, just as they can about a teacher or coach. Sometimes situations can become more complex; for example, when a stepdaughter sees herself and her mother as rivals for the stepfather's attention and affection and unconsciously or deliberately begins acting in flirtatious ways towards him.

Adults are expected to have the ability to exercise full responsibility for maintaining firm boundaries in their family relationships when it comes to romance and sexuality. Children and adolescents, on the other hand, may need help in appreciating and observing these boundaries. Sometimes stepparents may avoid dealing directly with the issue by treating it as a game; for example, responding to a flirtatious comment with a similar type of remark. While the stepparent may truly mean this in jest, the risk is that the stepson or stepdaughter may not hear it in this way. Fantasies that only contribute to the stepchild's confusion and ambivalence regarding new relationships probably need to be addressed openly and as quickly as possible. Whether it is the biological parent or stepparent who assumes the task, the child may need to be told as sensitively as possible that his comments or actions are inappropriate. As with many highly sensitive issues, emphasis on what is wanted and valued usually makes it easier to point out what is unacceptable. A stepdaughter who hears that her stepfather is glad she likes him and enjoys being with her will be more likely to accept his insistence that certain ways of speaking and acting should be reserved for a boyfriend.

8

Routines, Rituals, and Traditions

There is no better way of appreciating how important traditions are than by becoming a stepparent. There is also no better way of realizing how strange or even bizarre our traditions can seem to other people. What has been a normal and expected practice for years may be seen by the newly arrived stepparent as thinly disguised insanity. Take the Marshall Sausage Hike. It's a Thanksgiving tradition established when my first two children were young. The ritual is one my wife has struggled to understand, but has never shown the slightest interest in sharing after our first Thanksgiving together. From my perspective, we thoroughly enjoyed ourselves hiking through the woods while we collected the few dry sticks and leaves we could find. We searched for shelter so that a fire could be lit to roast the traditional English pork sausages for a picnic lunch. From Kathy's perspective, it meant leaving the comfort of a warm house filled with the aroma of a roasting turkey, walking through rain-soaked woods with people who would not even consider turning back if a cyclone hit, huddling over a poor excuse for a fire, and eating a piece of meat that was barely cooked beneath its charred exterior, all the time hoping she would be spared pneumonia and food poisoning. She has never joined us again. As far as I am concerned she has no soul; as far as she is concerned, we have no sense.

The Marshall Sausage Hike will live on; the new family has accommodated to the eccentricities of the old. Kathy too has brought traditions and rituals. Just thinking of Christmas alone, she has had an impact on how we open our gifts, what type of tree the gifts are found under, where the stockings are hung, the content of the meal, and the way the table is decorated.

Traditions and rituals make families feel there is a certain consistency and predictability in their lives; they also make them feel special and unique. Parents in nuclear families gradually establish their own traditions, combining aspects of each of their histories. Their children will be brought up with these traditions and will see them as an integral part of family life. Stepfamilies, on the other hand, run a greater risk of encountering a cultural clash. Traditions can sound trivial; after all, does it really matter if you have the Easter egg hunt before or after breakfast? But all it takes is someone to suggest that you change what has become an established practice for you to realize just how significant rituals are to you.

As a stepfamily forms, it can be entertaining to sit down and listen to each other's traditions. This is an exercise that can also be valuable in reducing the potential for conflict. Because people are so familiar with their rituals, they often assume that everyone must either share them or at least agree that they are the most appropriate. The early stage for a stepfamily, however, is to combine and adapt traditions, and sometimes certain habits may have to be broken. It seems that many books about stepfamilies return to issues concerning Christmas trees—perhaps because this season is so important to many people. A monumental sacrifice on my part was to agree to having a spruce instead of the pine I had been accustomed to seeing in the living room at Christmas for almost thirty years: one of us had to make a concession to avoid a standoff at the Christmas-tree lot.

Day-to-day practices also need to be discussed. Opinions regarding family meals, for example, can be widely divergent. For one family the supper table may be seen as the only time in the day when everyone is certain to be together. It is an opportunity to share an activity, talk about the day, air complaints and grievances, and discuss plans. Although most parents would not describe it this way, there can be a definite agenda. There may be the expectation that all members participate in the conversation, and parents will ensure that each child is asked a question about what happened that day. I was raised in a very different tradition. Children were fed after school. Parents ate later, on their own. This is a tradition I would like to reinstate, but Kathy is from the other camp and we have the mandatory half-hour of togetherness around the kitchen table. Occasionally I protest, but she pointedly reminds me of an article she read in which a *prominent* psychologist advocated the family meal as a way of facilitating communication in the home. As far as I am concerned the psychologist should lose his license; I'd also bet large sums of money he didn't have any children. So we gather every evening to communicate. The first ten minutes or so are spent trying to get a response that is longer and more informative than, "I don't know." Then, as the replies reach the level of whole sentences and the conversation shows signs of flowing, we counter with, "Eat up before it gets cold," or "Don't talk with food in your mouth."

I believe there are two critical attitudes to maintain when considering family traditions. The first is that there is no right or wrong; it is simply a question of habit and preference. The second is "Try it, you may like it," or at least not care one way or the other. I have not noticed any appreciable change in the quality of my family life since I agreed that the children did not have to ask if they could leave the table once they have finished eating. I also have to admit that Kathy's practice of opening presents in turn has added to the enjoyment of Christmas morning and eliminated the mayhem that tended to develop.

As stepfamilies become established, they begin to develop their own traditions. Sometimes these grow out of combining old practices; sometimes they are new. Some parents set themselves the task of creating a tradition for the family. This can sound contrived, but I prefer to see it as a way in which the stepfamily takes pride in becoming unique. Be it ordering a pizza and renting a movie on Friday nights, reading together after supper, or always stopping at the park on the way home from Saturday morning grocery shopping, having routine activities that include the stepparent can help everyone feel there is at least part of their lives that will be shared on a predictable basis.

9

How Many Families Live Here?

Most adults become accustomed to being members of at least two families at the same time. I am reminded of this whenever I participate in family reunions. Most of the ones I attend involve members of Kathy's family. I hasten to add that I have not been disowned by mine; they just happen to live over four thousand miles away.

Observing Kathy and her parents and siblings together never ceases to impress upon me how readily people can assume different roles in different family groupings. The five brothers and sisters are fully grown, independent, mature, and responsible adults who are very involved in their working and parenting roles. But at least part of the semiannual reunions is inevitably devoted to reasserting the old power structure and reenacting the sibling rivalries that have been unresolved for over thirty years. My younger brother-in-law has quite rightly no intention of ever totally forgiving his three older sisters for collectively deciding that oppression and domination were the best tools for building his character. My older brother-in-law, who recalls changing his younger siblings' diapers, still likes to point out when he feels they are making messes and offer advice as to how they should be cleaned up. What has changed is that the rivalry is almost always good-natured and is often staged for its entertainment value; there is none of the raw violence that used to arise as their childhood squabbles developed into furious arguments.

The reunions also remind me of the strength of family ties. There are times when I feel like an outsider—not because of being deliberately excluded, but simply because they want to spend time being their original family and I was not part of this shared history.

Most adult parents retain this membership in their family of origin. For those established in their own nuclear households, having different roles in the two families can feel very natural. In fact, the distinctions between the roles may rarely be articulated; people will move smoothly between one family grouping and another without ever having to consider who belongs or what role to take. Furthermore, with the decline in the number of households in which grandparents are living with nuclear families, it is likely to be true that a clear, physical boundary exists between the two groupings.

Stepfamilies and Blending

As always seems to be the case for stepfamilies, they have a more complicated situation to address. They have the additional task of deciding how many family units exist and establishing the membership list for each. In this chapter I will focus on the issue of the number of family groupings that can be present within a single home. In some instances, the home will be the primary residence of all the stepchildren; in others, all or some of the stepchildren will be living with the other biological parent and will be present only during access. Stepchildren's membership in the other biological parent's family will be addressed in the following chapter.

An illustration of the complexity of stepfamily life is when two single parents, both of whom have custody of their biological children, establish a home together. They will be starting with two separate groupings under one roof. The only deviation from this will be during periods when the children are spending time with noncustodial parents. Are these two families to remain separate or should they amalgamate and begin to see themselves as a distinct unit?

Before offering suggestions, I want to reintroduce the notion of "blended families." It's another one of those terms used in reference to stepfamilies that can lead to unrealistic expectations if it is applied too literally. My dictionary defines a blend as something that is, "mixed so thoroughly that the things mixed cannot be distinguished or separated." A major obstacle to such mixing in stepfamilies, however, is the closeness that often exists in single-parent families. Putting two such families under the same roof and expecting only one to emerge may prove to be a goal that is extremely difficult to attain. Relationships may develop and, over time, the stepfamily will acquire its own identity. At the same time, however, older children are particularly likely to retain the wish to see themselves as also belonging to the single-parent grouping.

I support the idea of dual citizenship when it comes to resolving the question of how to decide family membership. Just as people can move from being a parent in a nuclear family to being a sibling in their family of origin, they can shift between their roles in a stepfamily and single-parent family. Returning to the example of two single-parent families who begin living together, this means that some of the time there will be just one family, and at other times the two single-parent families will reemerge.

I have met with parents who have not only rejected the goal of blending, but have made deliberate efforts to preserve and respect the family units that existed prior to the stepfamily. In one home the routine after supper was for the mother to share activities with her biological children, while the father and his biological children went to another room to have their time together. Others have made a habit of scheduling outings that involve only the members of the single-parent family. Less formally, the understanding can be present that the children may want to be with or talk to their biological parent without the stepparent or stepsiblings being involved. My suggestion to parents is that any such wishes on the children's part not only be understood, but also be actively supported by creating opportunities for this type of interaction to occur.

Preserving the identity of a single-parent family can seem to be at odds with the development of a cohesive stepfamily. I do not believe this has to be the case; if anything, respecting the old family units can foster cohesiveness. Trying to insist that two groups blend can backfire; it can create either a façade of unity that eventually crumbles or precipitate outright rebellion as individual members of the household resist the takeover. Just as relationships between a stepparent and stepchild need to develop at their own pace, the emergence of the stepfamily as a distinct group cannot be demanded or prescribed. The attitude that people have the right and need to belong to different groups will often create the atmosphere of freedom and acceptance that encourages new relationships to be explored, rather than seen as potential threats to existing loyalties.

Although I have used the example of two single-parent

families living together, the issue of blending versus maintaining separate identities applies to many other stepfamilies. Another scenario is the stepfamily in which one parent has custody of the children from the previous marriage while the other has access to his. When the father's children are with the stepfamily, are they visitors or temporary, but full members of the family? Alternatively, should they and their father function as their own family grouping? Most stepfamilies will probably want the children to see themselves as more than visitors. Beyond this, flexibility is again warranted. The parents may need to have a planning meeting to consider the practical implications of such an approach. Will the father spend time just with his children? If so, how will this be balanced with his obligations to his stepchildren and wife? How can the children be involved in activities that will help them feel that they are part of the stepfamily? Will the activities include chores and other responsibilities, remembering the principle that part of feeling you belong to a group is knowing you are expected to pay membership dues? The result of tackling all these questions may be implementing weekend access that, in effect, involves the children's participating in two families, both of which will continue to have an important and independent meaning in their lives.

The stepparent who has no children of his own can have a struggle accommodating to the continuing existence of the old family. After all, when his spouse and her children function as a distinct group, he is left all on his own. I would like to do no more than offer my wife's view of this matter. When we were all living together as a stepfamily, there were occasions when just Joanne, Tim, and I would plan an outing that did not include Kathy. That left her alone in the house, coping with the solitude and temporary loss of both her husband and two adolescent stepchildren. Somehow she managed to contain her grief. "Punish me more often, why don't you?" summed up her attitude.

Unholy Alliances

Although asserting that it is generally healthy for members of the household to recognize that more than one family grouping will exist at times, there are situations in which preserving the old ties can be detrimental. If the prior family unit contains solid walls and boundaries that prove to be impenetrable, it can be impossible for the stepfamily to acquire an identity. The stepparent who does not have biological children and who establishes a home with a close single-parent family is most likely to feel excluded in this way. When this occurs, stepparents may report feeling as if they were still single and were boarding with the family. This situation is as unworkable as the extreme of insisting that the family function only as a total blended unit. It's like being invited to a party and finding out that no one wants to talk to you. I am reminded once again of the approach taken by my clinical instructor in family therapy. I specifically recall one of Libby's questions to a stepfather. She had noted how excluded he seemed to be in the sessions. His wife and stepchildren listened to his comments and politely answered any questions he might ask. Yet his talking seemed to interrupt the flow of conversation; the atmosphere became more formal and lacked the spontaneity and animation that were present when only the mother and her children were involved. Libby's question, "How long have you been knocking on the door, waiting for the family to let you in?" led to his beginning to talk about how lonely and isolated he felt, even though he had been a stepparent for almost four years.

Very strong alliances can exist that lead to the person's feeling he lives with the family rather than as a part of the family. To overcome such an obstacle it can be beneficial for the single-parent family to focus on the distinction between being *close* and becoming *closed*. The marital relationship is often pivotal in this regard. On the one hand, a stepparent needs to be open to becoming involved with his stepchildren; on the other, his partner needs to have the desire and trust to invite him to be part of her family life as well as her spouse.

Trends versus Goals

One reason why membership in family groupings remains significant for us is that we have an extensive and shared history with the other members. Whether contact with our family of origin is primarily a source of pleasure or leads to recurrent frustration, this contact is likely to be maintained. A history of living together that often spans two decades is obviously very significant in our lifetimes. Similarly, the history of the single-parent family can span several critical and eventful years and will be seen as another very significant period in the members' lives. As stepfamilies accumulate their own history, the importance and uniqueness of their family unit should also increase. Over time, stepfamilies may report that the prior groupings emerge less frequently; in the case of very young stepchildren, the old boundaries may disappear entirely.

These trends reflect the dynamic nature of stepfamilies; all family systems change and develop over time. But the difficulty encountered when trying to predict how stepfamilies will evolve should be reiterated. The view that the old boundaries will slowly but surely be eroded to the point where they no longer exist may prove to be another one of the unrealistic expectations that lead to unnecessary frustration. As will be discussed in the next chapter, stepchildren's membership in the other biological parent's family is likely to remain a permanent fixture in their lives. So too can their feelings of belonging to other family groupings that were part of their past.

I prefer to see removal of prior boundaries as yet another possible outcome, but never a goal. Returning to the topic of reunions, I accept that, while I am part of Kathy's extended family, I am also not a core member. They had a thirty-year head start and there will always be an important part of Kathy's life for which I can only be an observer rather than participant. She is in the same position when it comes to my history as a single parent. Even after twelve years as a stepfamily, Joanne, Tim, and I still head out for our own reunions; Kathy bravely continues the struggle to survive without us for the evening.

10

How Many Parents Do I Have?

One of the hardest tasks for divorcing parents is to separate as husband and wife while establishing a coparenting relationship that allows them to work together on issues concerning their children. With very few exceptions, the children will continue to want their parents together again. Although they can learn to accept that this will not happen, they typically maintain a strong wish to preserve their relationships with both. Furthermore, this wish will often be largely unaffected by the arrival of stepparents, even if the stepparent is in the home and spends more time with them than the noncustodial parent.

But is the child's wish to have a relationship with both

biological parents healthy, or could it be a sign of an inability to deal with the reality of the irreversible changes that have taken place in the family? How this question is answered has critical implications for the child. One school of thought has emphasized the latter interpretation. When a custodial parent has remarried, the stepfamily has been encouraged to close ranks so that the children can adapt more readily to the new home. Contact with the noncustodial parent and his family may be discouraged on the grounds that it is both disruptive to the stepfamily and confusing to the child. Intuitively, this line of reasoning has some merit. If you want children to become part of a stepfamily, why not immerse them in this new environment, rather than encourage them to maintain relationships that were part of the old, and now extinct, nuclear family? Another school of thought, however, has stressed the significance of the attachment to both biological parents. The advice to stepfamilies has been to treat the child's wish to have a relationship with the noncustodial parent as a need that should be recognized and met.

Fortunately there is research that can help stepfamilies take a position on this issue. Longitudinal studies of separated families have been conducted over the past thirty years, the most comprehensive being those of Dr. Judith Wallerstein and her colleagues in California. Children and parents have been assessed close to the time of separation and at various points after. These studies have added greatly to the understanding of the short- and long-term effects of separation. Part of the research tells us about the risks. For example, children of divorced parents can grow up to become very cynical about relationships. They may find it hard to trust adults, their self-esteem can be low, and their general social and psychological adjustment may be poor. Of interest, however, is that other children seem to survive the separation with little or no indication of any lasting, negative impact.

Given this range in how children are affected by separation, the crucial question becomes that of finding out what factors seem to determine the quality of adjustment following divorce. As is almost always the case in the social sciences, the results of studies that have looked at this question have two characteristics; they are not always consistent and they tell us that the situation is far more complex than might have been expected. In the midst of this inconsistency and complexity, certain trends are nonetheless apparent. One is that contact with the noncustodial parent does seem to be beneficial. More specifically, the quality of the relationship with the noncustodial parent, rather than simply the frequency of contact, has been shown to be related to children's adjustment. Those children who enjoy a high-quality relationship with this parent tend to show significantly better adjustment; unfortunately, Dr. Wallerstein found that under a third of the children at the ten-year follow-up (when a number were in stepfamilies) reported adequate or good relationships with the noncustodial parent. As a final note, she also reported that the psychological significance of this parent had persisted and often appeared to gain importance during the adolescent years.

There will always be instances in which contact with the noncustodial parent will not be beneficial—for example, if the parent is unable to offer a satisfying relationship with the child by virtue of extreme mental instability, problems with alcohol or drug addiction, or tendencies to be emotionally or otherwise abusive. For the majority of children in stepfamilies, however, a relationship with both parents is viable and can make a very positive contribution to their development. This requires coparenting—that is, sharing parental responsibilities with the former spouse so that children feel they can belong to the two families without being disloyal to either.

Obstacles to Coparenting

The ill-feeling and suspiciousness that often develop between separated parents can become a major obstacle to their working together on behalf of their children. I have become particularly aware of this during the custody and access assessments I have conducted. These are often requested by the court to help determine a plan of care for the children. Occasionally the parents are in the process of separating; more typically, however, the children are living with one or other of the parents or have become part of a stepfamily.

Approaches to this type of assessment differ; mine is usually to schedule initial appointments with the parents individually. In many instances I have found myself becoming increasingly sympathetic to the complaints of the first parent I happen to meet. By the end of the hour she may have convinced me that her ex-husband is as despicable a creature as ever walked the face of the earth. The litany of complaints and the accounts of wrongdoing are so compelling that it baffles me why she ever consented to marry such a villain.

When I subsequently meet the husband I wonder how he is able to present himself so well. I entertain thoughts that he must be a seasoned sociopath who lies just for practice. The more I listen, however, the more I start to become sympathetic to his view of the problems in the family and to his belief that he is reasonable, fair, and well-intentioned, while his ex-wife could not even aspire to such qualities.

In the face of such extreme and divergent viewpoints I have learned to place much weight on children's judgements. More often than not they will use words or play to communicate that both parents are fine people who are loving, caring, trustworthy, and attentive. They let me know about the special times they have had with their mother and father and also tell me how hard it is to understand why their parents seem to dislike or hate one another.

I want to stress that I do not believe most parents in separated families deliberately lie about one another. At the same time, a parent's perception of an ex-spouse is likely to be narrow or even distorted. Feelings of hurt, anger, and blame can prove to be persistent after the separation and will dominate and color how each partner sees the other.

Negative views of ex-spouses are likely to be particularly strong during custody and access disputes when parents have reached the point where it seems collaboration is impossible and the only way to decide matters is via a battle. It is nonetheless common for feelings of anger and bitterness to remain long after custody has been settled and the parents are formally divorced. Again Dr. Wallerstein's research is informative. She found that even after ten years of separation, almost half of divorced parents remained intensely angry at their former spouses. In principle, therefore, the idea that custodial and noncustodial parents should work together may be commendable. In practice, the continuing ill-feeling between them may make it seem anything but reasonable. Coparenting requires an alliance; most people asked to select a partner to work with on a project would not choose someone who evokes only anger.

Jealousy can be another powerful emotion that interferes with coparenting, as well as contributing to the anger felt towards the ex-spouse. A custodial mother may find that her standard of living has fallen substantially since the separation, while her ex-husband has the freedom and financial resources to enjoy the benefits of a bachelor lifestyle. The noncustodial parent, on the other hand, may be jealous of the mother's prominence in their children's lives. When his ex-wife remarries, the prospect of his children spending far more time with the stepfather than himself can lead to the fear of being displaced and heighten his feelings of jealousy.

Anger, resentment, hurt, and jealousy are not the only emotions that get in the way of coparenting. The term "emotional divorce" has been coined in reference to the distinction between legal and psychological separation. The parent who still has romantic feelings or fantasies regarding the ex-spouse may be legally separated; emotionally, however, the ties remain and can create difficulties for the stepfamily. A stepmother who senses this continuing attachment is unlikely to place her partner's ex-wife high on the list of people she wants to get to know. Chances are the ex-wife's presence will be seen as very threatening to the new marriage and family.

Sometimes it is the noncustodial parent who remains romantically attached to his ex-wife. Her involvement with a new partner may shatter most, but not all his hope of a reconciliation. The children may become a means of obtaining information regarding the new relationship. When children become messengers for this or other reasons, they usually feel very uncomfortable; they also tend to feel helpless, as refusing the request for information is to risk the disapproval of someone they want to please.

I do not want to overstate the potential problems. I need to remind myself that I usually become involved with families only when difficulties have arisen; obviously people do not arrange an appointment just to let me know they have no reason to see me. In a number of stepfamilies the stepchildren's contact with a noncustodial parent is both accepted and encouraged. It can also be the case that when it comes to the children, the biological parents have maintained an amicable, working relationship that persists with the support of any stepparents involved. I nonetheless would like to discuss those situations in which this type of coparenting relationship is not present and where children feel their loyalties are divided. For such children the price paid for having a relationship with both parents is to suffer the consequences of being caught in the middle of continuing battles and tensions that are not of their making.

Developing the Coparenting Relationship

I have developed a seven-part program for coparenting in stepfamilies. Its goal is simple: to increase the likelihood that the children will have a relationship with both their mother and father that does not burden them with adult problems and issues. The program makes a number of requests of parents, each one as unreasonable as the next. Only those who have been guaranteed that their lives will be rational or easy should dismiss the program out-of-hand. Because of its complete lack of consumer appeal, it is not available commercially.

1. Use Self-Inflicted Guilt

I like to take full advantage of the fact that parents care very deeply about their children and will want to protect them from potential danger whenever possible. Consequently, I have had sessions with stepfamilies in which I start by declaring my intention to use the children as a means of motivating the family to develop a coparenting relationship. I make no effort to disguise this shameless manipulation on my part as it often offers the greatest chance of success; it would make little sense to ask a mother and stepfather to adopt a course of action that might be extremely difficult for them if it were seen as being primarily beneficial to the ex-husband.

If I have met individually with the children, I may review what I have learned about their perception of the parents. Usually this involves my emphasizing how important and special both biological parents are in their lives. Just as I have done in this chapter, I then embark on a discussion of the findings and insights provided by Dr. Wallerstein and other clinical researchers. I use the "good news—bad news" approach. The good news is that children in separated stepfamilies do not have to be scarred by the losses they cannot avoid; the bad news is that, if parents are not careful, wounds can develop that are deep and painful.

Parents need to know the risks facing their children. I do not encourage them to wallow in guilt, but I assume that, as adults, they will expect to shoulder responsibility for the separation and, as parents, will hold themselves accountable for doing whatever they can to reduce its impact on their children.

2. Practice Voodoo

There are a number of parents who could blackmail me with the threat of disclosing my habit of prescribing bizarre ways of dealing with anger and jealousy. It would be impractical of me to ever advise that the parents and stepparents in a child's life all love one another, and I would never ask a biological parent to begin liking the ex-spouse. To the contrary, I encourage members of the family to acknowledge the feelings they have and recognize that emotions such as jealousy are normal and understandable. What I do ask, however, is that any negative feelings they may have towards an ex-spouse or stepparent be kept away from the children. One researcher asked stepchildren to identify the most stressful aspects of their family lives. Hearing biological parents talk negatively about each other was very high on the list, as was feeling caught in the middle of their parents' conflicts and experiencing obstacles to visiting the noncustodial parent. Whether shielding children from the negative aspects of their parents' relationship requires sculpting an effigy, painting a face on a pillow, or developing a stiff upper lip or ulcers is none of my business, as long as the anger is expressed behind closed doors.

I am not advocating deceit. Children are often aware of how their parents feel about each other and there would be little point in denying such feelings. The distinction between being *aware of* and *involved in* other people's emotions is the key issue here. Conveying the message to a child, "I know you love your mother and I want the two of you to continue to have a special and close relationship even though we don't get along right now," is promoting honesty and awareness. Allowing children to hear or witness the conflict directly, or sharing negative opinions about an ex-spouse with them, are examples of involving them unnecessarily. John and Emily Visher, who have written extensively on stepfamilies, summarize the importance of avoiding this involvement in the book, *Normal Family Processes:* "One of the greatest gifts that divorced parents can give their children is to leave them out of adult battles."

3. Distrust Your Instincts

The lack of communication that so often exists between custodial and noncustodial parents sets the stage for events to be misconstrued in a negative light. For example, there may be a good reason why a child returns home twenty minutes late from an access visit. If the reasons are not explained, however, the custodial parent may see it as yet another example of the ex-spouse's vindictiveness and unwillingness to abide by an agreement.

Assuming that you are wrong leads to consideration of alternative and benign explanations for what has happened. If a child states she has been disciplined by the other parent for no reason, try assuming there was indeed a reason, and one you would probably see as justified if only you knew what it was. It is normal for a child in any family to seek comfort and support from one parent after being reprimanded by the other; no one is particularly enthusiastic about being disciplined and we all like to find someone who will side with us. There is also nothing like selective reporting of the facts to elicit support for our cause. I recall my three-year-old complaining bitterly that she had been sent to her room for dripping water on the floor after her bath. Any sympathy I had for her quickly disappeared on discovering that certain details had been omitted, the most notable being her experiment to determine if a combination of vehement splashing and emptying out the entire contents of the shampoo and conditioner bottles would generate a bubble bath to be remembered. As it turned out, the experiment had been an unqualified success.

I do not want to suggest that children's complaints about the other parent should be totally dismissed; situations can arise in which children are being treated unfairly or inappropriately. It is nonetheless beneficial to retain the awareness that when the relationship between parents is poor, each is likely to side unnecessarily with the child against the other. Children often recognize this intuitively. Sometimes clinicians label this as manipulation on the children's part—that is, deliberately playing one parent off against the other. I prefer to see it as not so much a problem with the child's behavior, but more a reflection of a weakness in the system that has developed because of lack of communication between the parents.

4. Write a List of Your Ex-Spouse's Good Qualities

This list can be burned or swallowed before the ink dries, but its construction has value. Assume that your children have inherited a modicum of good taste (from you) and that they do not place people high on their most-favored list without justification. They may see qualities in both their parents that each has ceased to recognize in the other. A man may be given a failing grade as a husband, but keep his A rating as a parent. Trying to see him through his children's eyes is a difficult, but necessary part of understanding how important it is to support their relationship with him.

One mother even went so far as to think about the qualities her children had in common with both herself and her former husband. For the purpose of the exercise, only strengths and talents were listed. She then shared her conclusions with the children, resulting in a highly unusual, but beneficial version of, "You're just like your father."

5. Assume That You're Doing It Wrong

Parents can genuinely believe they are doing nothing to discourage their children's relationship with the other biological parent, even though their actions may, in fact, be creating the opposite effect. During my work with stepfamilies I often have occasion to explore the extent to which children feel they are caught in a crossfire between their biological parents. It is not uncommon to find that parents and children have very different perceptions of this matter. From the parents' perspective, they may believe that the children are not exposed to any negative feelings that exist. During the course of individual sessions with the children, however, they may complain loudly about the many ways each parent conveys dislike of the other. I recall a teenager telling me about a regular occurrence in her stepfamily that bothered her greatly. Lindsay was hesitant to talk about it at first as she said it sounded petty. It had to do with the way her stepfather or mother reacted when her father made one of his regular calls to talk to her. If her mother or stepfather picked up the phone, Lindsay knew immediately that it was her father at the other end. Just the way they stood and the tone of their voices told her that the phone call was as welcome as disease and pestilence. As they called her to the phone, she described herself feeling as if she were entering a battle zone. She was quick to point out that they never said anything derogatory; it was for this reason that Lindsay felt awkward about complaining directly to them. All they said was something to the effect of, "Hello. Yes, she's in," followed by, "Lindsay, it's your dad." The power of nonverbal communication, however, should never be underestimated. Without too much effort I'm sure you could read these lines to convey two very different messages. The first would be, "Lindsay's here and I'm sure she'd like to speak to you," followed by, "Lindsay, it's your dad. I'm sure you'd like to speak to him." The second would be, "Not you again. I knew we should have got an unlisted number," followed by, "Lindsay, if you want to speak to the jerk, go right ahead, but make it snappy."

Children can be asked to identify ways in which parents communicate their negative feelings about one another. Lindsay's mother and stepfather wanted to know how to help her feel less unhappy about the separation, and they also had the insight to recognize how they were conveying subtle, but strong and

93

unwanted messages to her. The family had a dramatic flair and the capacity to smile at themselves. This resulted in one session in which they role-played many different ways of answering the phone, as well as other situations in which Lindsay found their references to her father upsetting.

6. Lay Yourself Open to Rejection

If moving between the two families is like crossing a battle zone, this not only causes children stress, but also makes them feel powerless. They rarely know how to make peace, although most desperately want it. Peace negotiations need to be left to the parents and stepparents, and someone has to make the first move. The move can be modest and tentative and should be made at the time when your self-esteem is high and you can view risk-taking as a means of countering the humdrum of daily existence. The risk is simply that people who carry olive branches and white flags sometimes get shot, but at least you know you will survive and can applaud yourself for your heroism.

There are many examples that come to mind of parents who have implemented small, but significant changes that have helped their children immensely. One mother and stepfather always invited the father and stepmother into their home when the daughter returned from the weekend stay. They spent a few minutes talking together and the mother made a point of asking about aspects of the visit she knew the daughter would have enjoyed. Although the conversation was brief and superficial, it was civil and pleasant. It was also a welcome change for the daughter, who had finally been able to tell them how getting out of the car and walking up to the apartment on her own often brought the sadness and anger regarding the separation to the surface.

Another example of bridge-building was the stepmother who always asked if there was anything special they should know when she and her husband picked up the children. Often there wasn't, but the question communicated interest and respect rather than the coldness, or even disdain that can characterize such interactions.

Again, I am not advocating hypocrisy or deceit. "How wonderful to see you" is not required, and probably would not be believed if it ever passed the stage of being stuck in your throat. It may be that the former spouse or stepparent always remains someone you would prefer not to do business with; if so, just add them to the list of people you don't particularly like, but need to engage in a good working relationship.

7. Forget Consistency

The central premise of so many aspects of child-rearing is consistency. I'm usually a supporter of this premise; routines and discipline, for example, are hard to establish or put into practice if the parents in the home are not working together. The goal of consistency between parents in a nuclear family is facilitated by the fact that they live together and have ongoing opportunities to monitor what they are doing and discuss how they want to approach child-rearing. Separated parents obviously do not have this shared experience. Another factor is that families evolve rather than remain static. Separation leads to two different family units, each of which will evolve in its own way. As a result, stepchildren can expect to divide their time between two families that may be similar in some respects, but may also have unique and increasingly distinct characters.

The differences between families often come to the forefront in the area of discipline: what is acceptable behavior in one home may be outlawed in the other. Children may also bring to light differences in privileges and material benefits. One parent may think nothing of giving children money to go to the store or taking them to a movie; the other may not have the financial resources or desire for such generosity.

In most instances the starting point I recommend is to assume that different rules and practices are just that—alternative ways of running families, neither of which is necessarily better or worse than the other. From this perspective, striving for consistency between the two households is unnecessary and may only serve to generate aggravation and frustration as one parent asserts that his approach is correct and should be followed, while the other takes a similar stand.

An argument against accepting the differences between the homes is that it will be confusing for children. If the contrast is extreme, perhaps this would be so, but children in any family typically become accustomed to dealing with a variety of standards. As they grow older they become increasingly aware that the families they may visit can have widely divergent policies and practices. They can also try to take advantage of this fact at opportune moments, reminding parents, for example, of the large number of children they know who never have to look at, let alone eat a vegetable, and are allowed to stay up much later than they are, usually for the purpose of counting the vast sums of money they are given for their allowance. Many parents will point out that the survey has omitted the cash-poor vegetarians who are in bed by seven. During such discussions I also like to remind my children that, while some of their friends may have had the good fortune to be born into wonderfully kind and indulgent families, they have been condemned to live with mean and miserly parents who are too old and stubborn to change.

Children's awareness of differences between families is accompanied by an ability to accommodate to the household they happen to be in at a particular time. My nieces and nephews can stay with us and adapt quickly to our routines and expectations. When our children spend a day with friends and receive return invitations, I assume that they have learned and followed at least some of the most important rules. Children in stepfamilies can also accommodate to the fact that one household has more liberal rules regarding television-watching than the other, or that their mother insists they drink all of their milk at supper while their father is more permissive at the meal table, but a stickler when it comes to putting away their toys before bedtime.

There can be exceptions. When stepchildren are very young, feeding schedules and nap times will require a degree of consistency between the homes. Older children might experience difficulties that call for the parents to work particularly closely together. I recall a custodial mother and stepmother who jointly implemented a program to help their son overcome his reading problem. As he frequently spent time with his father and stepmother, it was felt that responsibility for the program had to be shared if it were to be effective. Children may go through periods when consistency will prove most important to address certain behaviors. For example, if parents are helping children overcome problems such as lying, stealing, or recurrent bed wetting, having a shared plan of action carries a better chance of success than operating in isolation.

In most situations, however, I encourage stepfamilies to accept and support the differences that exist and to refuse to feel defensive when children point out the inconsistencies. Periodically it may be necessary to explain that every family has its own way of conducting business and that, unless they are being asked to do something that is potentially harmful, you want them to respect the other parent's opinions and authority. Beyond that, endless debate is hazardous to your health. A look of stony indifference is called for if you are yet again hearing, "But Dad lets us...." You might also add my favorite standby, "Tell someone who cares"; this has helped me survive many situations in which further discussion is pointless.

Coparenting and Remarriage

Coparenting focuses on the needs of children in stepfamilies. While giving children priority may be warranted, the possibility that contact with the former spouse will have a negative impact on the new marriage needs to be considered. Some studies have examined the correlation between the amount of contact with the former spouse and the degree of marital satisfaction in the stepfamily. The study reported by Doctors Weston and Macklin from New York is particularly relevant. The general trend was for greater contact to be associated with higher levels of marital satisfaction in stepfather families. They also demonstrated the importance of considering the extent to which the couple in the stepfamily is in agreement regarding the type of relationship that should exist with the former spouse. In situations where the couple was clearly at odds when it came to how much communication or direct interaction there should be, this conflict tended to override the general trend and led to dissatisfaction in the marriage. When the couple had been able to reach an agreement, on the other hand, this added to the quality of the marriage and typically reflected the fact that both the mother and stepfather wanted to have a positive relationship with the father.

Weston and Macklin talked generally about how the structure of stepfamilies does not have to predispose them to failure. They emphasized that couples can work towards reaching consensus regarding the coparenting relationship and stressed the importance of so doing. Although their study looked specifically at stepfather families, a quote from their paper would almost certainly apply to all stepfamilies: "The good news is that couples can create a successful remarital relationship while allowing for a high degree of wife coparental involvement with the children's noncustodial father. Unhappily, this kind of continued coparental involvement does not appear to happen very often."

11

Stepmothers

For a while it was hard to decide if I should devote a whole chapter to stepmothers without giving equal space to their male counterparts. Then it struck me that stepmothers and stepfathers have never been treated equally, so why should I break with tradition? Stepmothers have been singled out as the recipients of one of the most unfavorable stereotypes in our society. What adds insult to injury is that the woman's motive is rarely to become a stepmother. If you set your sights on becoming a tax auditor, debt collector, or politician, you know you are volunteering for a low standing on the popularity polls. But the job of stepmother is one that is thrust upon the woman by virtue of her husband's history rather than any wish for instant motherhood.

Just as unavoidable as the job, is the negative image it has evoked for centuries.

The Wicked Stepmother Tradition

Marriage is supposed to bring at least a smattering of joy and happiness. It's one of those major steps that are expected to add to the quality of life. Of all the people who get married, however, women who simultaneously become wives and stepmothers are the most likely to be in for a rude awakening and feel somewhat cheated. What can make it even more frustrating for them is that remarriage seems to work the other way for their husbands. Men tend to be happier in remarriage than they were when single; for women, it's the opposite. I should add that this is most likely to be the case during the early years of remarriage; the situation often improves as time goes by. The usual caution regarding trends also has to be noted, as not all stepfamilies by any means will conform to this pattern. But, overall, it is stepmothers who seem to find that the quality of their lives has gone down.

One of the difficulties facing stepmothers is the negative press they attract. The reputation that precedes them is far from flattering. Of all the adjectives at our disposal, "wicked" is the one most strongly associated with the title. This is obviously not a good start when it comes to a job description, but it does reflect how stepmothers have been portrayed in our society in general and children's literature in particular.

Cinderella is a case in point. She simply needed a mother to love and care for her. Her father was a pretty good merchant, but he was a failure when it came to picking out potential mothers. He married a woman who was proud and haughty; she proceeded to dress poor Cinderella in rags and treat her like a servant. Her stepsisters (who were also very mean, and ugly to boot) joined in the act, and if it hadn't been for the intervention of a fairy godmother and Prince Charming, Cinderella would have been condemned to a life of drudgery.

Cinderella was not alone. Hansel and Gretel and Snow White also had problems adjusting to stepfamily life. The culprit was the stepmother; each one was mean and cold. Hansel's and Gretel's stepmother was a particularly nasty piece of work. Her solution to the fact that they were low on groceries was to abandon them in the woods, where they almost fell victim to cannibalism.

As a stepchild in a fairy story you could hope for eventual retribution, but you could expect to endure many years of persecution before justice would be done. Snow White's stepmother, for example, did have to wear red-hot slippers and dance to her death, but only after her poor stepdaughter had fled murderous soldiers, been a skivvy for seven diminutive miners, and eaten a poison apple.

Cinderella Revisited

Charles Perrault wrote *Cinderella* long before the emergence of social scientific research. Presumptuous though it may be, I have taken on the task of rewriting his story in light of the studies that have been conducted into stepfamily life.

Cindy had been living alone with her father for many years. He was a kindly soul who loved his daughter dearly and wanted nothing but the best for her. Alas, his work in sales often took him away from home and Cindy would be left on her own.

Over the years Cindy grew used to life in a single-parent family. In fact, she found herself becoming closer to her father and liked having him just to herself when he was at home. But when he thought of his daughter alone at home, with her only source of cultural stimulation that of reading the instructions on the TV dinner, his eyes would fill with tears. Oh how he wished Cindy could once again have a mother to love and care for her; then his life would be complete.

Just after Cindy's fourteenth birthday he went to a far-off city for a sales convention. There he met the second woman of his dreams; a lady so fair and charming that he knew at once that his prayers had been answered. He fell to his knees: "Give up your career this very day, sell your house tomorrow, and move in with me and my adolescent daughter." It was an offer no woman could refuse.

When Cindy met her stepmother her emotions were mixed: resentment and distrust in equal portions. Her stepmother's smile and cheerful greeting were met with an icy stare, as was taking Cindy to her volleyball practices, ironing Cindy's blouses, and serving tuna casserole. "Just give it time," said her husband, who was now going to many far-off cities, safe in the knowledge that his daughter was being well taken care of.

"I am not trying to be her mother, am I?" thought Cindy's stepmother to herself as she was spending yet another evening preparing the supper and helping Cindy with her homework. "I don't want to be the heavy," she added to herself as she once again reminded Cindy of the house rule that dishes had to be done before the mold became visible. "Help! I am being turned into a Wicked Stepmother," she lamented, as she was met with the now familiar, "You can't tell me what to do, you're not my mother" and "You're treating me like a servant."

The story doesn't end here, but I haven't worked out all the details yet. There's a dance Cindy goes to wearing her stepmother's brand-new outfit, a sixteen-year-old boy with a motorcycle she meets there, an all-hell-breaking-loose crisis as she misses her twelve o'clock curfew by three hours, and a final scene where the stepmother is being interviewed by a sociologist for a study into parental satisfaction during the first few years of remarriage.

Nobody's position in the stepfamily is easy. At the same time, it often seems that stepmothers are in a particularly difficult position. While gender stereotyping may be less pronounced than it has been in the past, the majority of women remain more involved in childcare than their spouses. Stepmothers can feel pressured by their own expectations into assuming more responsibility for their stepchildren than will a stepfather. This pressure can also come from their spouse and from society at large. In some families this can result in the stepmother almost immediately taking on the role of the primary caregiver; there is no time for the gradual integration into the home and the slow and careful assumption of parental responsibilities that are known to help stepfamilies become established.

Wicked stepmothers are made rather than born. The negative image associated with their role is created by unrealistic expectations and demands; the solution requires a negotiation of roles in which the father supports his wife's status in the family while respecting the fact that the process of creating new parent-child relationships can take many years.

The Wicked Stepmother Scale

Just in case you are not convinced, I have constructed a WSM scale designed to identify mothers who are, by nature, prone to abandoning their stepchildren in dark forests whenever they run out of milk and bread.

WSM Scale

1. I am overwhelmed by feelings of inadequacy and failure whenever I hear my stepchildren saying something nice about me.
2. As a child I could never understand why Cinderella's step-mother had not been canonized.
3. I encourage my husband to work long hours so I can have his children all to myself.
4. At night I dream of new and creative ways to make my stepchildren feel miserable.
5. Being a stepmother is an ideal way to release all my repressed and primitive feelings of hostility.
6. Before reading this book, I thought "wicked stepmother" was meant as a compliment.

7. If I had written children's fairy stories, Snow White would have got the red-hot slippers and Cinderella's stepmother would have been a shoo-in for the glass ones.
8. I dread the days when my stepchildren will leave home and I will have no one left to persecute.

If you have answered "yes" to more than three of the items you are entitled to use the letters W.S.M. after your name; more than five and there is a good chance you will be featured in a fairy tale sooner or later.

A Note of Optimism

Let me return briefly to the current research. When groups of young people have been asked to rate mothers-in-general and stepmothers-in-general, the results typically conform to the stereotype; the respondents provide a more positive description of mothers than they do stepmothers. But there are two other findings I would like to discuss. The first is that the expectation that stepmothers will be rated more negatively than stepfathers is not being found consistently. Perhaps this reflects a welcome shift away from gender-role stereotypes. The other finding is that stepchildren rate the stepmother role more positively than do children from nuclear families. This is also encouraging. It suggests that the negative assumptions a person may have of a stepmother will be lessened rather than intensified by the experience of actually living with one. Familiarity does not have to breed contempt; in fact, one study found that approximately three-quarters of stepchildren felt they had developed a close or moderately close relationship with their stepmothers. This figure rose to almost 90 percent when just stepdaughters were surveyed.

The fairy stories will continue to be told and I doubt that too many children will be hearing my version of Cinderella. These fairy stories, however, reflect a small, minority position; stepmothers do not have to follow such scripts.

12

Stepsiblings

Introducing a stepparent into a child's life can be demanding; when the stepparent has children, the instant creation of stepsiblings adds to the challenge. My first contact with the Reynolds family was yet another reminder of how there is a world of difference between putting things together and actually mixing them. Marilyn and Gerry had been single parents. Marilyn brought two preadolescent daughters to the stepfamily; Gerry had one son and a daughter—both teenagers. It was one of those situations where it was easy to tell which members of the stepfamily were biologically related. Gerry's children sat either side of him: Marilyn's sat with her. The way the stepfamily interacted also highlighted the boundaries. When Marilyn spoke, her daughters were alert and contributed, while Gerry's children adopted a trancelike pose that let everyone know they had no interest in the proceedings. Gerry's speaking, however, seemed to function like an on-switch for them. They immediately showed signs of life and would contribute to the conversation, although none of their comments were directed to their stepsisters.

When I asked if the division between the families was typical of their day-to-day lives, I was informed that the children were being remarkably well-behaved. It was as if they had all agreed to an uneasy truce for my benefit; at home the standoff would usually be followed by a major eruption.

The family taught me a great deal about stepsiblings. Over the following months I had the opportunity to gain an understanding of each stepchild's views and feelings, both through family and individual sessions. Each had their own reasons for resisting the idea that they should become a sibling group of four.

The oldest was Gerry's son, Martin. He was a quiet, thoughtful sixteen-year-old who shared his father's interest in classical music, reading, and tennis. He was a conscientious and capable student and, although Martin was not especially outgoing, Gerry praised his choice of friends. In fact, Gerry praised his son for many things and with good cause. His only complaint was that Martin sometimes forgot to keep his room clean. As my children never remembered, I was left feeling amazed and inadequate and endeavored to find subtle ways to learn Gerry's secrets while maintaining my image as the professional.

Martin was not impressed by the arrival of Marilyn's children. He had one sister and felt that was more than enough for anyone. He had a real fondness for his sister, Beth, but did not go out of his way to make this known. More often than not they went their separate ways, not because of any hostility between them, but because they had different interests and friends.

To Martin, Marilyn's children had done little more than add to the congestion in the bathroom and the noise level in the house. He told me he would have been willing to talk to them, but would find it difficult to carry on a conversation about figure-skating, pop music, or designer clothes.

Martin was looking forward to graduating and was beginning to make plans for a career. What concerned him was that the single-parent family he had known for years was no longer present. As a result, he would be growing up and leaving a family that was changing rapidly and to which he could never feel he belonged fully. In so many words, he highlighted the dilemma facing many adolescents who enter a stepfamily—that is, how to reconcile developing relationships with new family members with the need to separate and become less dependent on the home.

A final and important issue for Martin was that he had always enjoyed the time he spent with his father. He liked being with his friends, but his father was still his preferred partner for going to a concert, playing tennis, or discussing the latest book he was reading. Although he had not voiced his complaints directly, he resented the amount of time his father seemed to devote to his stepdaughters. He had listened when his father explained how important it was that he show his interest and affection for all the children. Martin understood his father's position, but this did not mean he had to like it.

Beth had just turned thirteen and it was obvious that living with her would never be boring. She hovered between being articulate and self-confident on the one hand, and plain mouthy on the other. She was a reasonable student, but probably could have done better. Her teachers made comments about her need to apply herself more fully and concentrate on the academic aspects of classroom activities so that she could demonstrate her potential. Roughly translated, this meant that she'd get higher grades if she used her brain more and her mouth less.

I stress Beth's outgoing and assertive nature, because it contributed to the problems between herself and her stepsisters. The parents were in the process of building an extra bedroom in the basement, but in the meantime the three girls had to share what had been Beth's room. Actually, as far as Beth was concerned, it was still her room. She made no secret of her opinion that it was her territory and her stepsisters were invaders. She blamed them entirely for the fact that her desk had been taken out to make room for bunkbeds and that drawer space was at a premium.

Beth also found it embarrassing to share the bedroom. She was well into puberty and did not like changing her clothes in front of two younger, and sometimes curious, girls. Her efforts to ban them from the room as much as possible met with strong opposition and little success. Her father stated repeatedly that it was *their* room, and Beth was left without an ally in her campaign to repel the invaders.

Like many thirteen-year-olds, her position in her peer group was high on Beth's list of priorities. The unspoken rules for group membership rendered it impossible for her to even consider counting her stepsisters as friends. She could see no obvious role for them to play in her life that would be of any value or interest to her. When I asked if she ever enjoyed their company, the only concession she made was to acknowledge that she had occasionally spent time with her younger stepsister, Anne, that was "okay." Anne was eight years old and liked to ask Beth to help her with such things as choosing her clothes and brushing her hair. Sometimes Beth had even read to her at night when her mother was working late.

Laura had just turned twelve and epitomised the displeasure and frustration experienced by deposed older children. As a member of the single-mother household she had been number-one child. Being the first-born may have certain disadvantages, but you do tend to have more power and privileges. It is part of the human condition not to want to relinquish either. Not only was she no longer number one, she was not even second-in-command in the new pecking order. She was trailing behind a stepbrother whose status included being in high school and working towards his driver's licence, and a stepsister who was in her teens and was allowed to wear make-up and go to school dances.

Beth's presence, in particular, was a constant reminder to Laura of her lost position. Martin tended to ignore her, but Beth would make her very aware of their different ages; she also liked to find any excuse to utter her favorite comment, "You're so immature." Pushing this button was all that was needed to bring their rivalry to a head. It usually resulted in yelling matches, but occasionally they had become embroiled in physical fights.

My suspicion that Laura had a crush on Martin was never confirmed, but I think I was probably right. She envied his being the oldest, but also seemed to be developing a sneaking admiration for him. The way she talked about her two stepsiblings was so different. When the subject was Beth, she did not even try to hide her frustration, anger, and jealousy. Her stress level subsided noticeably, however, when Martin became the topic of conversation, and she even went so far as to state that if she had to have an older brother, he would be acceptable. If my theory is correct, she had a definite soft spot for Martin, but his apparent disinterest in her led to her reluctance to try to close the distance between them.

Anne's favorite two words were "not fair." Being the youngest of the four was not fair; neither was having the smallest allowance and the earliest bedtime. Not fair also applied to having to go to a sitter after school, never being allowed to spend time at the mall without a chaperon, and not having a choice about going to church. But above all, Anne felt cheated when it came to her relationship with her biological parents. Beth and Martin saw their biological mother regularly. She had remarried, but always made a point of setting aside regular and often long periods of time to see them. They had an annual vacation with her, she phoned frequently, attended their special functions and events, and never forgot a birthday. Anne's father, on the other hand, had become increasingly uninvolved in her and Laura's lives. This was partly because his work had led to his relocating and the round trip of several hundred miles would make frequent visits impractical. Still, as she pointed out, he could phone more than he did and his efforts to see them were few and far between. Most damaging for Anne had been his many, but usually empty promises to her. Primarily through her mother, she had let it be known that she wanted to see, or at least hear from him, more often. He would show an interest for a while, but the good intentions he expressed never translated into sustained action.

Not having much involvement with her father was probably one of the reasons Anne developed such a close and dependent relationship with her mother. Sharing her mother with two stepchildren was not an attractive proposition for her. As far as she was concerned, Martin and Beth had a father and mother; she only had a mother. It was obviously not fair for her mother to pay attention to them; they already had a lot while she had so little.

Anne had mounted a campaign to keep her stepsiblings and mother apart. Although I do not believe she sat down to actively plan how to do it, she was utilizing behaviors that young children often exhibit when they want people to respond to their needs for affection, closeness, and attention. She was regressing. Thumbsucking, coming into her mother's and stepfather's room complaining of a bad dream, and using baby talk were examples of behaviors that had begun to occur regularly. It was also guaranteed that if Marilyn were involved in an activity or conversation with either of her stepchildren, Anne would find some way to intervene. Interruptions, pretending to be hurt, climbing onto her mother's lap, or starting a fight with her sister were all ways in which she had diverted attention back to where she felt it rightly belonged—herself. The campaign was only partially successful. She was usually able to become the center of attention, but at the cost of annoying others. Anne was not concerned about aggravating her stepsiblings, but her mother's approval meant a lot to her and was becoming less frequent the more she acted up.

Martin, Beth, Laura, and Anne were not bad or disturbed children. They just saw very little advantage to doubling the size of the sibling group and found plenty of reasons to complain. These reasons are not difficult to understand. In nuclear families there will be the occasional child who will pester his parents to give him a new brother or sister, but how many sixteen-year-olds put in two such orders? And human beings, like many animals, are highly territorial. If you have your own space you tend to defend it vehemently; it is a rare person, for example, who would welcome sharing her office if she had enjoyed having one to herself for years. Similarly, not wanting to accept a lower position in a pecking order is as understandable as the president of a company not wanting to trade places with a junior executive. Continuing the parallel with the working world, expecting Anne to accept her new position can be compared to asking the junior staff to take a pay cut while the bosses get a hefty raise.

The Reynolds family was not, in my experience, an extreme example of the problems that can arise. There can be situations in which a stepbrother or stepsister is readily accepted or even welcomed. Whether in the home permanently or visiting on weekends, a stepsibling can be a wanted playmate and companion and an attachment can develop that proves to be close and strong. The majority of stepfamilies that create stepsiblings, however, can expect to encounter obstacles and resistance between the two sets of children. The task becomes that of surviving the stress, tension, and open conflict that often develops and helping the children accept and benefit from the new family structure.

For the Reynolds family, just the process of talking about the problems was of great survival value. As I have discussed in reference to other issues facing stepfamilies, it can be very difficult to know how much change will be possible. If only for practical reasons, therefore, the first goals need to be those of understanding and at least partial acceptance of the current situation.

Over a period of time, each of the four perspectives on being a sibling was explained. As well as the children speaking for themselves, they were encouraged to guess what it might be like to be in someone else's place. Martin, for example, was surprised and interested to find that Anne had such a rose-colored view of what his life must be like. She listened intently to his version, equally as surprised and interested.

Part of understanding and accepting the problems encountered by stepsiblings is acknowledging that a state of peace and harmony between brothers and sisters is not the norm in any type of family. Some may achieve this, but many of us can recall lengthy periods of sibling rivalry. This is a matter that was discussed by the family, with Marilyn, Gerry, and myself recalling aspects of our personal histories. I remember that, at the age of six, my brother allowed me to become a junior member of his Skill Club. This meant I had the fourth spot in the line as we ventured out into the woods, blazing new trails, climbing trees, and riding our bikes everywhere except on the designated paths. The next act of kindness I recall is when he offered to help me pack after I threatened to leave home as a teenager. I carry no bitterness. As a bratty younger brother I had no equal and I do not doubt that I deserved much more than I got. Much to my mother's chagrin, it wasn't until we were entering adulthood that West and I began to establish the civil and close relationship we enjoy today. I like to think we weren't that abnormal. Stepsiblings have their own special reasons for viewing one another as rivals, but they also share the competitiveness that can be part of any family.

Gaining a fuller understanding of the conflict between

stepsiblings and accepting it as normal is a necessary part of survival, but it is unlikely to be seen as sufficient. Stepfamilies will want to move on; they may abandon the objective of a total blend or mix, but will expect more than a permanent standoff. The Reynolds family tackled this problem in a number of ways. We had one session when it was the parents' turn to stay in the waiting room. The task was to see if the rest of us could come up with a plan for the four siblings not to have to live together as a group. Having decided that none of them wanted to live apart from their respective parents, the only remaining solution would be to plot to undermine the marriage. Beth quipped that marriage licenses should be renewable, just as they are for cars and dogs, and that her father and stepmother should be refused an extension. Fortunately, this was no more than a fanciful notion and there was no doubt she recognized that the marriage was very important to her father and was there to stay. In the face of the fact that they were condemned to live with one another for several years, the choice was between an out-and-out battle for supremacy, a permanent cold war, or an attempt to find some midpoint between a truce and peaceful coexistence.

One of my reasons for writing about the Reynolds family is that my contact with them spanned a number of years. They returned on more than one occasion. This was partly because of the parents' view that having periodic "checkups" was a good idea for the family. They also asked me to help with career and educational planning for two of the children; this gave me additional opportunities to inquire about their progress as a stepfamily.

Certain developments might have been predicted. Beth began to like being a big sister to Anne. She became something of her teacher, babysitter, and friend, all rolled into one. Anne looked up to her, shed a few tears the day she left home, and could not wait for her first opportunity to visit her overnight.

Gerry and Marilyn talked of the frequent discussions they

had as a couple about the relationships they felt could be fostered. Recognizing that Beth was at least partially receptive to Anne's seeking attention from her led to their encouraging this type of interaction. Wisely, they avoided applying any pressure to bring them closer together. It was more a question of making sure they thanked Beth whenever she had taken on even a very minor responsibility for Anne's care. They also let her know whenever Anne had told them about an enjoyable time spent with her. Of all the stepsibling relationships, theirs had probably been the most rewarding. It seemed that, as far as both girls were concerned, each had gained a sister.

Beth and Laura were a different story. Laura never appeared to accept losing her position as the senior child and most of her resentment was acted out in her relationship with Beth. Marilyn was careful to ensure that, as the older of the two biological sisters, Laura continued to have privileges and rights that Anne would have to wait to be granted. More generally, though, it became a question of trying to enforce a truce between Beth and Laura. The two girls became part of regular negotiations as to what were acceptable and unacceptable ways of behaving towards one another; they also had a say in deciding consequences for violating the terms of the treaty. At best, they learned to tolerate one another. As happens between biological siblings, this could, of course, change for the better in adulthood, but I felt Marilyn and Gerry had accepted the limits of the girls' relationship and did not see this as a sign that the stepfamily had failed in any way.

Gerry decided to sacrifice most of the limited time he had spent in leisure activities outside the family. During the three years before Martin went to college, Gerry set aside time for them to be together. Beth was not ignored, but her need for such involvement was less. In fact, Gerry remarked that he was lucky if an arrangement they made did not end up being broken because she had a more appealing offer from a friend.

The parents told me how they also modified their expectations regarding Martin's involvement with his stepsisters. Labels can sometimes be helpful and they chose to use "cousins" as the one that came closest to describing the relationship of Martin to Laura and Anne. The extra attention Gerry paid to his son probably paved the way for Martin to see his stepsisters less negatively and eventually form a largely amicable, although never close relationship with them. Marilyn and Gerry tried to create opportunities for them to be together, again without applying pressure. One particularly creative maneuver was letting it be known that Martin would rarely be denied the opportunity to use the family car if at least part of the driving involved transporting his sisters for their various appointments and activities.

As Laura and Anne grew up, their interests also changed and more of a common ground between themselves and Martin became apparent. When they all happened to be under the same roof, they seemed to like being together, although they rarely took the initiative to seek one another's company.

I came to know Marilyn and Gerry well enough that I could ask questions for the sole purpose of satisfying my personal interest. I was curious to know how their experiences in a stepfamily measured up to their hopes. They did not hesitate to talk about the disappointments they had felt, particularly in the first few years. They wanted to have a very close family and were reluctant to give up the idea that somehow all four children could form a tightly knit unit in which distinctions between steprelationships and biological relationships would disappear. It was difficult to accept that this idea would never be more than a fantasy. Marilyn, however, described how eventually recognizing this as a fantasy also brought a sense of relief. They did not have to try so hard to be close, and they did not have to contend with the frustration and self-reproach that went along with measuring themselves against unrealistic standards. They also made an observation that was unexpected. Each had worked hard to reassure the children how special and how important they were, and would remain. As a result, they found themselves expressing their feelings towards the children more frequently and more openly. Their own childhoods evoked mainly positive memories, but both wished their parents had been equally as demonstrative.

13

Grandparents

The Supportive Role of Grandparents

I never knew my grandfathers, but I am fortunate to have fond memories of my two grandmothers. In retrospect, the qualities I appreciated most in them were their ability to overlook my faults and liberally dispense warmth, love, and cookies. They were not naive or imperceptive; they were fully aware of my many imperfections, but knew there were plenty of other people willing to point these out to me.

My reasons for feeling my grandparents were special and important were by no means unusual. Greg Kennedy at Central Missouri University asked young adults about their recollections of the grandparent to whom they felt particularly close. There were many reasons given for this closeness, but the grandparents were typically portrayed as caring people who were fun to be with and who showed a special interest in them. The grandparents' ability to understand them, and their willingness to provide encouragement and a sympathetic ear were also high on the list. For some, it was the feeling that the grandparents had treated them as individuals that was foremost in their memories. And in spite of the years that had passed, many continued to have much admiration for their grandparents and still placed value on earning their approval.

We all should have someone in our lives who fits the above description, and there are times when this type of close and supportive relationship will be especially important. The period after a separation is one example. Children find that day-to-day life no longer seems as predictable and consistent as it used to be. Too many things start to change too quickly. There is the prospect of moving and having to make new friends. They may not know what type or relationship, if any, there will be with the noncustodial parent, and the anxiety regarding what life will be like in a single-parent family can be high. At times of stress and uncertainty, it is always reassuring to have someone who can be relied on and whose position in your life will be constant. It is often a grandparent who can fit this job description.

Kennedy's research is of interest here as he found that adult stepchildren recalled their relationships with grandparents as having been particularly significant. When compared to adults who had remained in nuclear families, the stepchildren's memories of the affection, attention, and support the grandparents had provided remained particularly strong and probably reflected the fact that in a number of instances, the grandparents had become more involved in their lives following the separation.

Unless there is a compelling reason not to do so, I recommend that every effort is made to maintain children's relationships with all their biological grandparents. If the respective families have taken sides following the divorce, maintaining contact with former in-laws can place great demands on the parents' ability to separate their own feelings and wishes from those of their children. A mother's painful experiences and memories regarding the marriage may lead her to want to have as little as possible to do with anyone associated with her former spouse. Contact with his parents may also be very awkward if they hold her responsible for the separation. The approach I suggest is much the same as that described for developing a coparenting relationship with a former spouse. However difficult it may be, I encourage parents to make sure that any anger or resentment they may harbor towards former in-laws is not allowed to overshadow the wishes and needs of their children. These negative feelings may be understandable, but children can be upset and confused if they are exposed to emotions that are so contradictory to their own.

I also recommend that parents are vocal in letting their children know that every effort will be made to preserve their relationships with all their grandparents. It is often a good idea to communicate this intention to the grandparents as well. If face-to-face contact feels uncomfortable, a letter may be called for; whatever form of communication is used, the statement of intent can be a powerful means of allaying the fears that both children and grandparents can have about the future of their relationship.

The stepparent can have a crucial role as well. Grandparents may see the arrival of the stepparent as a potential threat to their relationships with the grandchildren. This is especially likely to occur if the separation led to the grandparents becoming more involved in the children's care. As a result, grandparents may expect the transition from a single-parent home to a stepfamily to undermine their position in the children's lives. To some extent it is inevitable that their role will change as the mother and her new spouse begin to share responsibility for the children. But becoming less prominent in a grandchild's life does not have to mean becoming redundant. The few minutes it will take a stepparent to let the grandparents from both sides of the family know that he understands their importance to the children can prove to be a very worthwhile investment. It can create the expectation that there is room for everybody—that a new person can become involved in the family without challenging existing relationships. From this standpoint, the stepparent's arrival is a process of addition, not displacement.

Stepgrandparents

There was a time when family trees took care of themselves. They grew in a more or less predictable pattern. The odd branch might wither, but for the most part, the branches spread out symmetrically. Divorce has wreaked havoc with this orderly growth and family trees are now rearranged with abandon. Divorcing parents may favor radical pruning as they attempt to distance themselves from one another. When a stepfamily is formed, on the other hand, the prospect of grafting a whole new branch onto the tree is created by the presence of the stepparent's extended kin. But whether or not the two families wish to be joined in this manner is an issue that can be hard to resolve. For example, when a father has a son who marries a single mother, are her children to be seen as his daughter-in-law's children or his grandchildren? Applying the latter label may feel awkward, if not inaccurate; it typically implies an emotional attachment that is highly unlikely to be present. The myth of instant love again becomes relevant. Just as stepparents' lives are made much easier when this myth is dispelled and they can feel free to allow relationships with their stepchildren to develop at their own pace, stepgrandparents need the same freedom with their stepgrandchildren. Encouraging some involvement, such as inviting stepgrandparents for family dinners and exchanging cards on special occasions, can provide opportunities for relationships to develop. It is important, however, not to create pressure for this development to occur.

I also believe this is an area in which a great deal can be accomplished by way of building family cohesiveness without monumental effort or commitment. One stepgrandfather I met decided to host a barbecue for the sole purpose of welcoming the children and introducing them to other members of their extended stepfamily. Part of the proceedings was to show the children pictures of their stepfather when he was a boy and tell the accompanying stories from his childhood designed to cause him at least some embarrassment. I was struck by the effect this welcoming party had on the mother. It had been long-remembered as the event that convinced her she was accepted into the family. She realized that her children had status, even though they did not have biological ties to this part of the family tree.

The difference in how grandparents are likely to feel towards a biological grandchild and stepgrandchild is hard to ignore when both children are living in the same home. This difference, however, does not have to be an insurmountable problem. Most children can understand that grandparents who have known their grandson from birth will want to spend more time with him than with a stepgranddaughter they did not meet until she was eleven. If she is close to her own biological grandparents it can be easier for her to understand and accept the special relationship between a stepsibling and his grandparents. When this closeness is absent, however, there is greater potential for jealousy to develop and greater need for all concerned to be sensitive to how she is likely to feel.

Differences in attachment only tend to become major problems if they are accompanied by open or subtle rejection. A girl who stays behind while her stepbrother leaves on an outing with his grandparents can be hurt and upset if she feels ignored. The stepgrandparents' greeting her warmly, however, and taking a few moments to show some interest in her, will reduce the likelihood that she will see herself as a second-class citizen. Jealousy can also be lessened if the stepgrandparents offer to include her in at least some of the activities. At a later stage, the distinction between biological grandchildren and stepgrandchildren may diminish. On the other hand, the distinction may always remain, particularly if the children are older when the stepfamily forms.

I am reminded of how my first two children's relationships with their stepgrandparents have evolved. Tom and Grace were initially "Kathy's parents" who happened to be there when we came together for family functions. Over the past twelve years, however, they have become far more than Kathy's parents; by the same token, Joanne and Tim have become far more than "Peter's children." I am uncertain as to when the changes took place and I cannot recall ever having discussed them. Evidence that they are real, however, is not difficult to gather. It was never an issue deciding if Tom and Grace would be invited to Joanne's graduation; it was obvious they should. And when they sent a care package to Tim after his hospitalization we shared his pleasure, but were not surprised.

Help and Hindrance

There are two complaints about grandparents that I hear most often from stepfamilies. Both have to do with acceptance. The first is that a biological grandparent does not accept the stepparent; the second concerns rejection of a stepgrandchild.

Difficulty accommodating to a stepparent can be attributable to several factors. One is fear of the unknown. The new person may have no proven track record as a parent, no strong attachment to the children, and the negative image that is conjured up by the title "step." Such characteristics may fail to impress grandparents who have a lengthy history with the children and may have become increasingly involved with the family after the separation. Comparing the stepparent to the previous spouse can also be an obstacle to acceptance. It may be very hard for a stepmother to fill the shoes of a former daughter-in-law who was held in high regard by the grandparents.

The parents of the former spouse can also have their own reasons for reacting negatively to a stepparent. A stepfather who lives with the children may have no difficulty accepting that their relationships with their paternal grandparents should be encouraged. The grandparents, however, may resent the fact that the stepfather is living with the children and seems to be occupying the position that rightfully belonged to their son.

When a stepparent is rejected, both the biological parent and the children can be caught in the middle of tension and conflict that have the potential to be highly destructive to the stepfamily as a whole. The message that the stepfather is not good enough can be transmitted in words or actions and places the wife in a position where she feels torn between her husband and her parents. The children are also likely to develop at least some awareness of the division between the families. They can come to see their grandparents as people who will readily listen to any complaints they might have about the stepfather and who will automatically take their side and perhaps intercede. He can opt for as little involvement as possible with the children and his new in-laws, but it is hard to be content in a family if you feel you are a non-voting member whose presence is, at best, tolerated. This situation will become particularly stressful if the mother seems more strongly aligned with her parents than with her new husband. He may begin to see her as more their daughter than his wife; this inevitably places strain on the marriage.

Rejection of stepgrandchildren has the same potential to be divisive. Parents' love for their children and their wish to protect them are likely to be the strongest motivating forces in their lives. This translates to, "Mess with my kids and you're messing with me." If you feel your children are being unnecessarily hurt by someone, it would be improbable that you would sit idly by; in most situations, you would also want your spouse to support you.

When relationships with grandparents or stepgrandparents are becoming a source of stress for the stepfamily, the first avenue to be explored—and explored thoroughly—is always discussion and negotiation. I also encourage stepfamilies to start with the assumption that problems have arisen without there necessarily being any evil intent. There may be some grandparents who deliberately plot to act in ways to undermine the stepfamily, but I suspect they are few and far between. Most have the same lack of familiarity with stepfamilies as is true of the majority of parents. Most also share some of the feelings of anger, uncertainty, and anxiety that are so often associated with separation and remarriage. Working from the assumption that intentions are not as negative as they may seem can make it easier to both explain the problems the stepfamily is experiencing and remain optimistic that the situation can be changed for the better. Once again, placing emphasis on what is wanted, rather than focusing on complaints, is usually most productive. A mother who can find a quiet moment to talk to her parents and explain how their support is important to her and needs to include supporting her new husband may encounter a receptive audience; waiting until either she or the stepfather is so frustrated that a particular incident triggers an angry confrontation is likely to lead to resistance.

The starting point is to be clear regarding what is wanted. Parents in a stepfamily may want to take the time to talk together to decide how they would like to be treated. Whatever form this may take, the underlying principle is usually no more than the expectation that each person in the family will be treated with respect and sensitivity. From this perspective, it is more than reasonable for parents to seek change when they feel this respect and sensitivity is lacking. Suggestions can then be made. Grandparents can be asked to tell their grandchildren to refer complaints back to the management rather than siding with them against the stepfather. A stepgrandmother can be told just how much difference it would make if she spent a few moments talking to her stepgrandchildren or possibly bringing them a modest treat when returning her biological grandchildren from an outing.

When negotiation fails, the choice becomes difficult. A mother who feels caught between her husband and her parents can opt to accept the situation, but the stress this entails can become intolerable. The alternative is to take a stand. Sometimes this requires closing ranks and establishing that the stepfamily has certain expectations that will have to be met if the grandparents are to be actively involved with the children. People in this situation may find it difficult to take such a strong position with their own parents. It can be helpful to be reminded that it is normal for families to reach temporary impasses. There are occasions when relationships become strained because family members take a strong position that they refuse to relinquish. While it may be more traditional for the parents to be the ones laying down the law, a reversal of roles never hurts. In most instances, the strength of the ties that exist in the family will eventually bring about the changes needed for the children to develop positive relationships with their grandparents.

14

Yours, Mine, and Ours

More Children?

At the age of seventeen my ambition was to be a poet. I envisaged a Bohemian lifestyle and decided I would have no wife and no children. At the last count I was at two and five respectively. I hasten to add that I have no wish for either tally to increase. When my children ask why I wanted to have five of them, my standard reply is that I kept hoping that sooner or later one would turn out all right. As is so often the case, they don't take me seriously, but the question remains unanswered. I am not so narcissistic as to believe I have a duty to make as large a contribution as possible to the world's gene pool. In order to receive an allowance, my first-born had to sign a document outlining how she will take care of me in my golden years, so I did not need more children to increase the likelihood that one would provide this service.

In retrospect, probably the main reason for our large family is that my remarriage was one of the many examples of how a couple in a stepfamily can be at very different stages in their lives. I had two children who were halfway through their childhoods, and the thought of giving them a sister or brother never entered my mind. Like many adults, I came from a society in which two children per family was the norm, and I was quite satisfied to have met my quota. More often than not I felt content in my role as a parent; at the same time, the prospect of Joanne and Tim becoming adults and leaving home before I turned forty-five was known to put a faint smile on my face.

Kathy was a different story. As a single young woman with no children, she was in that period of life when family involvement is minimal and priority is given to building a career and just having fun. Then she married me. Marital bliss lasted until we pulled into the driveway after our brief honeymoon. Although being greeted by two children signaled the resumption of a family life of which she was very much a part, Kathy retained the wish and drive to proceed through other stages that are a part of many women's lives. She wanted the experience of giving birth to a child and the opportunity to become closely bonded to an infant who would be in her care throughout childhood. Fortunately, the idea of expanding the family did not become an issue of contention, and three "mutual children," Aaron, Kiera, and Alexandra, followed.

Many parents in stepfamilies find themselves at different stages of the life cycle, particularly when one has children and the other does not. Ideally, the question of whether or not to have children of their own will be a matter that is resolved prior to the marriage. In some ways, this is no different from the planning any couple should undertake before deciding to marry. Discovering that your spouse views pregnancy as a yearly event, while you break out in hives at the mere sight of a child, would obviously herald a major problem in the relationship. The ques-

128

tion for a couple who are thinking of forming a stepfamily is essentially the same—is it important for them to have a child (or more children) of their own? Reaching consensus, however, may be harder. I have no regrets, but it took a while to get used to the idea that I could be slipping out of Alexandra's high-school graduation early to make it to my retirement party. For this and other reasons, the husband or wife may have serious reservations about adding to the family, and I have met couples in stepfamilies who have come very close to separating because of their divergent wishes. One problem is that the matter can hardly be settled through compromise; you either have a child or you don't. For these couples, saving the marriage meant that one person had to radically rethink goals and accommodate to the partner without harboring resentment and bitterness.

Beyond exploring their wishes and priorities as a couple, parents in a stepfamily are faced with the complex task of determining the likely impact of a mutual child on the family as a whole. Will the children feel they have become unimportant to the stepfather now that he has a child of his own? Will the stepfather feel guilty if he finds his emotional attachment to his biological child is far greater than to his stepchildren? If the father's children visit rather than live in the home, will they feel jealous of the fact that their new half-sibling is with him all the time?

The problem with such questions is that prediction in this area is so difficult. There is no point asking a person such as a psychologist, as you won't get a straight answer. I could make a case for leaving things alone; it's tough work establishing a stepfamily, so why make it even more complicated? I could also make a case for adding another member to the household. A stepfamily consists of different parts, and truly bringing them together is a slow process. Why not have a child that everyone is related to; a focal point that makes everyone belong?

If forced to get off the fence and offer a hint of direction, I would argue that having a mutual child can be very rewarding. Emphasis would be on *can*. The research tells us that a mutual child is not a guarantee that the quality of stepfamily life will increase, but neither is it necessarily associated with a decrease. The only outcome you can be sure of is that the relationships within the stepfamily will be altered. If change is anticipated and care is taken to consider how each person may react to the baby's arrival, the addition to the family can prove to be positive for all concerned.

Impact of Mutual Children

Almost all parents are somewhat surprised at the extent to which their first child affects their lives. While a mutual baby is obviously not the first child, her impact can nonetheless be strong. The structural differences between nuclear and stepfamilies are relevant here. A stepparent with no biological children at home will often have a very different position in the family from his spouse. He may take only minimal responsibility for the day-to-day care of the stepchildren and his role in discipline may be minor. He may not be seen by the children as having a strong parenting role and may not himself seek such status. Becoming a father of a newborn, however, immediately changes the situation. It is no longer a question of having to decide how much involvement, if any, he should have as a parent. He has full legal right of guardianship, with all the expectations and responsibilities this entails.

The relationship between the husband and wife will almost certainly be influenced by this development. Previously the husband may have been a backroom consultant when it came to the care of the children. Now he is likely to be a full partner who shares authority equally with his wife when matters concerning their child are involved.

Just as it can take time for any new parent to adjust to the demands and responsibilities of caring for an infant, other members of the stepfamily can find themselves confronted with unexpected and perhaps unwanted changes in the way the family operates. Andrea was eleven when her mother and step-father had their first mutual child. She was very pleased and excited before her half-brother Kevin was born. In fact, there was a strong family history of multiple births and she had been hoping for twins. She was, however, alone in her disappointment that the ultrasound revealed a single occupant.

Marty had been part of the family for nearly two years and felt he had a good relationship with his stepdaughter. Almost all the parenting, however, remained his wife's responsibility. Jackie had raised Andrea as a single parent for over six years and their relationship was very close. Andrea was also an easy child to manage and it suited the family well that Marty took a peripheral role. Over the period they had been living together, he and Andrea had definitely become friends, and there was every indication that their relationship would become stronger. At this stage, however, he did not have the degree of authority, influence, and attachment that typically goes along with the title "father."

Shortly before I met Andrea, she had become increasingly withdrawn. She was also argumentative and sulky, which was out of character for her. Jackie and Marty were particularly perplexed by her angry outbursts, which included threats to run away and live with her father. While she had regular contact with her father, she had no memory of living with him and had never expressed a wish to do so previously.

Andrea consented to my using dolls during our individual sessions. She was a mature preadolescent, but agreed not to let it be known that I played with dolls if I afforded her the same confidentiality. Her arrangement of the figures representing members of her family had a distinct pattern. Whether depicting a scene in the home or acting out a fantasy such as being shipwrecked on a desert island, the grouping that emerged most

131

strongly was mom, stepdad, and Kevin. At one point I put the dolls representing herself and her mother at opposite ends of the table. Andrea placed them side by side to show me how close she wanted them to be. She created a large gap, however, when asked how close she felt they actually were. The question, "Is anyone between them?" led her to immediately position her stepfather in the middle. It seemed that Andrea had no doubt in her mind that she was no longer very important in the family and that her only hope of improving the situation was to convince herself and her mother that a transfer to another home was in order.

As Andrea became more verbal about her complaints, I was reminded of how events and situations that might otherwise be unremarkable or trivial can assume great significance in stepfamilies. She talked about how she had wanted to be there when Kevin was born and complained that not only did she have to wait several hours before seeing him, she had not been able to hold him until he came home. And the issue of holding him had remained a thorn in her side. She could only do so with permission. Asking her mother was not a problem; accepting that Marty had such authority was a different matter. As far as Andrea was concerned, Kevin should be first and foremost her own and her mother's baby.

In some respects Andrea's perception of the reorganization in the family was correct. Marty had a lot more power, along with a lot more sleepless nights. He took his job as a parent seriously, and there would be many occasions in a normal day when he and Jackie were focusing their attention on the baby. For Andrea, however, it was a lot more than just the amount of attention focused on her brother. She was able to understand, and largely accept, that babies take more of a parent's time than an eleven-year-old. For her, it was more a question of feeling the family had reorganized in such a way that she and Marty had switched positions. Before Kevin's arrival, it would have been Marty who might be left out; now Andrea found herself in the backseat.

Comparing her own and Marty's old and present positions was one reason for Andrea's difficulties. Another was comparing her and Kevin's relationship with Marty. She liked her stepfather and knew he liked her, but that was far removed from the warmth and love that seemed so obvious from watching him and Kevin together. When he talked about his son, Andrea remarked it was like Kevin was the "only baby in the world." While he was also very special to her, her brother's closeness to Marty made her feel that her own relationship with Marty was insignificant. To some extent she blamed herself for this. Although she was certain that Marty loved Kevin more than he cared about her, she also believed Marty would have been willing to have a closer relationship with her than had developed to date. They had often talked as a stepfamily, and Marty had emphasized that he was not going to try to force a relationship with Andrea; he would let her set the pace. This had undoubtedly been a wise approach, but with Kevin's arrival Andrea began to wonder if she should have set a quicker pace.

As for Jackie, she liked the fact that Kevin provided the opportunity for her and Marty to work together as parents. She much preferred having her husband as an equal partner to the more distant role he had with Andrea. This also allowed her to see a side of him that had not previously been demonstrated. Although she fully expected him to be a good father, seeing proof of this on a daily basis made her optimistic that they would have a successful family together.

Of all the members of the stepfamily, Marty was the most vocal in talking about how his view of family life had changed. Being a parent to Kevin might be exhausting at times, but it was much simpler than dealing with the complexities of stepfamily relationships. He did not have to worry about whether or not he was doing too much or too little, and he did not have to reassure himself that, given time, the relationship would probably become closer. When it came to Kevin, the attachment was immediate, and he went ahead and did what needed to be done with confidence.

Andrea did not have the opportunity to live with her father. Her mother and stepfather decided to treat this issue as one of those totally-out-of-the-question requests. She was told in no uncertain terms that her home was with them and that the family would not be a family without her. I suggested to Andrea that she make every effort to be as obnoxious as possible to make them change their minds, and even gave her a few tips from my own childhood. Thankfully she decided such efforts would be pointless; she had heard and believed her mother's and stepfather's commitment to her.

Over the course of several months, the problems that followed Kevin's arrival seemed to dissipate. It is often difficult to pinpoint the reasons for change, but several factors were probably instrumental. Marty earned his wings as a parent and Jackie began seeking his opinion more often regarding Andrea. At the same time, it seemed that Andrea was beginning to see him more as a parent. She still deferred most matters to her mother, but the occasions on which she chose to involve Marty were becoming more frequent. No attempt was made to mask the fact that Marty felt differently towards Kevin than Andrea; neither was it denied that Andrea felt a closeness to her mother that she did not share with her stepfather. But as well as defining the limits of their relationship, they talked about picking up its pace and they set aside times in the week that were just for them to be together.

The issue of Andrea's having to seek permission to hold Kevin was resolved indirectly. Jackie and Marty decided they were being far too protective and that Andrea should be recruited as a part-time, junior parent. She took great pleasure in learning how to look after her brother and his care became something that was shared among the three of them.

The impact of the mutual child will vary from stepfamily to stepfamily. For some the effect will only be positive. Because of the ages of the stepchildren or the length of time the stepfamily has been in existence, the distinction between biological parents and stepparents may be minimal. As a result, the new arrival may not lead to any major change in the stepparent's position and power in the family or present such a threat to existing relationships. In such families, the child's welcome can be unequivocal.

When both parents already have children, the mutual child creates the "mine, yours, and ours" family. In this type of stepfamily there is no expert and no novice when it comes to parenting; although the husband and wife are both stepparents, they also have their histories of being biological parents. The stepchild may not, therefore, have the task of forming a new image of the stepparent.

While the type of stepfamily may have an influence on how the mutual child is received, generalizations are hazardous. The "mine, yours, and ours" family, for example, may contain two credible and experienced parents, but it also has two sets of children who can find themselves reacting differently to their half-sibling's presence. If the mother's children are in the home, accepting the baby may be fairly immediate and straightforward. But if the father's children only visit on alternate weekends, for example, knowing that their contact with their new brother or sister will always be far less than their stepsiblings' can cause resentment, jealousy, and rivalry.

A starting point for parents is to think in terms of domino, or ripple, effects. Try to imagine how each person, including yourself, might react when the baby arrives. Part of this can be very concrete. Whose routines will change? Who will have to spend time with the baby and who will receive less attention as a consequence? Whose position is likely to change and, in particular, is anyone in for a promotion or demotion? How is each person likely to view the baby—long-overdue sibling, tough competitor, a bit of both, or perhaps no more than someone whose arrival will go largely unnoticed? Will there be changes in how the members of the family see one another? Will having a common half-brother or -sister help stepsiblings feel connected to one another, or are the personalities and circumstances such that rivalries are likely to develop? Is there a risk that the stepchildren will see the stepfather as someone who is stealing their mother's attention if he begins to work closely with her in caring for the new baby?

Parents in many families will spend time preparing children for the arrival of a sibling. For stepfamilies, the need to do this can be particularly strong and is accompanied by the parallel need for the adults to prepare themselves for the changes that can occur in their positions and relationships. Sometimes it is helpful to assume that there will be at least someone who will feel threatened or insecure. This may sound like encouraging people to find problems where none may exist, but I prefer to see it as preventive. The mutual child has the advantage of immediately having a place in the lives and hearts of parents; a nuclear family is created around the baby, in which emotional attachments and strong relationships are as guaranteed as they can ever be. The baby will, however, be in the midst of a more complex family system in which some of the attachments and relationships can be ambivalent, tenuous, and fragile. Working on this assumption can begin the process of parents' finding ways to assist individual family members to adjust. One child may need to be reassured that he will not be any less important or loved; another may respond enthusiastically to the prospect of being given responsibility for the baby's care. Yet another may need to hear that her feelings of ambivalence regarding the baby are understood and accepted. A general discussion about how life in the home will be different can also assist family members to anticipate change and not feel confused or insecure when it occurs. Return on the investment of time and effort can be substantial. Just the process of talking together lets everyone know that, while the baby's arrival is a very special event, all members of the family deserve consideration. Parents may find that some of their expectations regarding how others in the family will react to the mutual child are wrong. I doubt that this matters. The fact that they have communicated their interest and concern will help establish a climate in which problems can be voiced when they arise and feelings can be expressed openly, rather than acted out in ineffective and possibly damaging ways.

15

Rewards and Strengths

Stepfamilies are hard work. They require inordinate patience, effort, insight and commitment, and my task is to convince you that it's worth it. I could appeal to the Puritan ethic; the more you put into something the more you get out. Like many of my generation I was brought up to believe in the value of hard work. My parents tried to convince me that I would not appreciate things if they were handed to me on a silver platter. But as much as they were probably right, I would have liked the opportunity to find out for myself. At school, the Air Force motto hung everywhere: "Per Ardua Ad Astra." My Latin never exceeded pitiful, but a rough translation is, "more pain, more gain." But the more they tried to convince me that pain and suffering built character, the more I became willing to leave mine in a sorry state of repair. It would, therefore, be blatant hypocrisy if I tried using either the Puritan ethic or theories regarding the value of pain to persuade you that stepfamily life is rewarding.

It also strikes me that talking about the rewards of stepfamilies can seem like rampant rationalization if all you are experiencing at the moment are the punishments. Is there really any solace and comfort to be had?

To begin with, one of the free benefits that can be included in your membership in a stepfamily is a crash course in advanced communication skills. There are so many issues and potential hazards to consider and, in most instances, stepparents do not have the benefit of prior experience to help them feel confident that they know how to deal with them effectively. The parents and children need to learn how to express their thoughts and feelings about family life; they will also need to learn how to listen to the thoughts and feelings of the other members of the family. Parents will learn to take the lead in creating a climate in which everyone feels it is safe to raise sensitive issues and voice differences of opinion. Communication skills are, of course, important in any family. The days when parents stayed together for better or for worse are long gone and trusting the development of a nuclear family to instinct or natural evolution would be foolhardy. But stepfamilies are confronted with this reality at the outset; you cannot be lulled into a false sense of security when there are three days out of four when it seems that the options of sinking or swimming are equally probable.

The stepfamily is also an ideal environment for acquiring negotiation skills. For a child in a nuclear family there is an implicit understanding, for example, of what it means to be a daughter, sister, or granddaughter. The same child entering a stepfamily, however, can find herself suddenly becoming a stepdaughter, stepsister, and stepgrandchild. While these titles are easy to apply, actually knowing what they mean is a different matter. It is not simply a question of looking up the definition somewhere; roles have to be negotiated. What it means to be a stepdaughter, for example, will depend on what she and her stepparent need and want. It will also depend, in part, on the expectations, wishes, and feelings of other members of her family—such as both of her biological parents. And the effect of time has to be considered. Relationships rarely remain static, but those within stepfamilies have remarkable potential to change. At the age of six, the stepdaughter may see a stepmother as an intruder; at sixteen, the possibilities include polite acquaintance, arch enemy, friend, big sister, and mother.

As members of the stepfamily learn how to negotiate and modify their roles, they become aware of the range of potential relationships between people. The need to work hard to build these relationships probably accounts for those studies finding that stepchildren can have particularly well-developed social skills. I would not be at all surprised to hear that research with adults in stepfamilies comes up with similar results. Parents who take on such tasks as building a coparenting relationship with someone they would prefer never to encounter again, who spend years forging ties with stepchildren who can be hesitant, resistant, and openly hostile, and who can simultaneously make a marriage work, deserve to give themselves credit as well as an extended vacation. Such accomplishments require the person to develop their capacity for patience, sensitivity, optimism, and determined effort to its fullest.

My belief that stepfamily life has its rewards is also based on personal experiences. My hope that having a license as a psychologist would grant me immunity to the problems that members of a stepfamily can face proved to be yet another unfulfilled fantasy. It took a long time, for example, before I could truly appreciate the need to be flexible and accommodating. Now, after twelve years of being in a stepfamily, I believe I have become less self-centered. At one time I didn't know I was self-centered. When you are a single parent and responsible for making all of the decisions that parents typically make together, there is little need to accommodate or compromise. Entering a stepfamily and finding that you are living with someone you want to stay with, but whose expectations, wishes, and feelings are different from your own in many important respects, brings you face to face with the reality that calling yourself partners does not guarantee compatibility. For example, Kathy is many important things to Joanne and Tim and she has enriched their lives immensely, but they do not share the depth of attachment to one another that my history created. Intellectually, I was aware of the myth of instant love, but in retrospect I could not have accepted it emotionally. At some level I must have believed that the difference between how we felt about the children was a problem that would be corrected when she came to her senses and appreciated the golden opportunity she had to become a member of *our* family.

The idea that members of a home can operate as different family groupings at different times took some getting used to. I must have equated success as being "one big happy family." Experience taught me I could either accept that stepfamilies are different and more complex than their nuclear counterparts or waste my time by trying to insist that we conform to a simpler, more traditional model of family life. I suppose that I could have taken a stand and declared that either we all go on the sausage hike or we all stay home, but there is no doubt that the outcome would have been the loss of a cherished tradition that deserves to survive for generations.

I do not believe I have a rose-tinted view of stepfamily life. Kathy has read every line and would not let anything by that she felt was too far removed from reality. I can also recall periods in our history when the thought of writing a chapter about the rewards and strengths of stepfamilies would have been comical if it had not been for the fact that it's hard to smile when your survival as a family seems in jeopardy.

The increase in divorce over the past few decades has led to the stepfamily becoming commonplace. As a result, it is less likely to be seen as necessarily inferior and a poor imitation of the "real thing." The prevalence of the stepfamily does not imply that the nuclear family is an outdated model; like my in-laws, we are not recommending to our children that they place "divorced with children" on the list of necessary characteristics for a potential mate. But if they make us instant stepgrandparents, I hope they will share my confidence that, although they may have to work harder to achieve a high quality of family life, this goal will be within their reach.

Suggested Reading

For Children:

"What Am I Doing in a Stepfamily?" Claire Berman and Dick Wilson. Carol Publishing Group, 1992.

Now I Have a Stepparent and it's Kind of Confusing. Janet Stenson and Nancy Gray. Avon Books, 1979.

What Kind of Family is This? A Book About Stepfamilies. Barbara Seuling and J. Ellen Dolce. Weston Publishing Co. Inc., 1985.

Mom and Dad Don't Live Together Anymore. Kathy Stinson and Nancy Lou Reynolds. Annick Press Ltd., 1984.

For Adults:

American Stepfamilies. William R. Beer. Transaction Publishers, 1992.

Step-by-Stepparenting. A Guide to Successful Living with a Blended Family. James D. Eckler. Betterway Publications, Inc., 1988.

How to Win as a Step-Family. Second Edition. Emily B. Visher, Ph.D., and John S. Visher, M.D. Brunner/Mazel Publishers, 1991.

Second Chances. Men, Women and Children a Decade After Divorce. Who Wins, Who Loses - and Why. Judith S. Wallerstein and Sandra Blakeslee. Ticknor and Fields, 1989/90.

Index

About the Author

Dr. Peter Marshall is a father of five, a child psychologist, and a resident of Barrie, Ontario. Born in England, he has lived in Canada since 1973. He has worked in the field of psychology for the past twenty years as a university instructor and later as a practising clinician, and has appeared on radio and television discussing his views on sexuality, assertiveness, and teenagers. Peter Marshall is the author of the highly successful *Now I Know Why Tigers Eat Their Young*.

STEINGARD PHOTOGRAPHY